OWNERS AND
NEIGHBOURS IN
ROMAN LAW

OWNERS AND NEIGHBOURS IN ROMAN LAW

BY

ALAN RODGER

Quae lucis miseris tam dira cupido?

VIRGIL

OXFORD
AT THE CLARENDON PRESS
1972

Oxford University Press, Ely House, London W. 1

GLASGOW   NEW YORK   TORONTO   MELBOURNE   WELLINGTON
CAPE TOWN   IBADAN   NAIROBI   DAR ES SALAAM   LUSAKA   ADDIS ABABA
DELHI   BOMBAY   CALCUTTA   MADRAS   KARACHI   LAHORE   DACCA
KUALA LUMPUR   SINGAPORE   HONG KONG   TOKYO

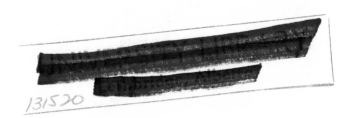

PRINTED IN GREAT BRITAIN
AT THE UNIVERSITY PRESS, OXFORD
BY VIVIAN RIDLER
PRINTER TO THE UNIVERSITY

FOR
DAVID DAUBE

PREFACE

THIS book is the revised version of a thesis submitted for the
degree of D.Phil. of the University of Oxford in June 1970. Little
account has been taken of material appearing after that date. In
any event I have not sought to cite all the relevant literature. Where
it is necessary, the rest can be traced easily through the works to
which I have referred.

While writing the thesis I was fortunate to hold the Faulds
Fellowship of the University of Glasgow and the Dyke Junior
Research Fellowship of Balliol College, Oxford. I am grateful to
both these bodies for their assistance. I did a disproportionately
large amount of the work in 1968 and 1969 while staying in
Münster, Westphalia, where I used the library of the Institut für
römisches Recht. During two summers of rain and sunshine,
Professor Dieter Nörr and all the members of the Institut made me
feel at home. I cannot thank them enough.

Professor Nicholas and Professor Stein examined the thesis,
Professor Stein undertaking the labour of re-reading a portion of
the draft for publication. Both made useful suggestions of which I
have taken account. Professor Honoré also gave me the benefit of
his criticism. Mr. D. N. MacCormick provided invaluable assistance of every kind. My thanks go to all these people. My principal
debt, however, is to Professor Daube who fought every inch of the
way with me. It is in affectionate remembrance of those skirmishes
across the fireplace in his rooms in All Souls that I dedicate the
book to him.

ALAN RODGER

New College Oxford
1 October 1971

CONTENTS

ABBREVIATIONS

Beseler, *Beiträge* 1–5

G. von Beseler, *Beiträge zur Kritik der römischen Rechtsquellen*, vols. 1–5 (Leipzig or Tübingen, 1910–31).

Biondi, *Cat.*

B. Biondi, *La categoria romana delle 'servitutes'* (Milan, 1938).

Biondi, *Servitù*

B. Biondi, *Le servitù nel diritto romano* (2nd edition, Milan, 1954).

Bonfante, *Corso*

P. Bonfante, *Corso di diritto romano*, vol. 2 1 (Rome, 1926).

Buckland, *Textbook*

W. W. Buckland, *A Textbook of Roman Law* (3rd edition edited by P. G. Stein, Cambridge, 1963).

Daube, *Aspects*

D. Daube, *Roman Law: Linguistic, Social and Philosophical Aspects* (Edinburgh, 1969).

Glück, *Ausführliche Erläuterung*

D. C. F. Glück, *Ausführliche Erläuterung der Pandekten* (edited by H. Burckhard and others, Erlangen, 1790–).

Grosso, *Servitù*

G. Grosso, *Le servitù prediali nel diritto romano* (Turin, 1969).

Grosso, *Usufrutto*

G. Grosso, *Usufrutto e figure affini nel diritto romano* (2nd edition, Turin, 1958).

Ind. Itp. and *Suppl.*

Index interpolationum quae in Iustiniani digestis inesse dicuntur, 3 vols., and *Supplementum* (edited by E. Levy and E. Rabel, Weimar, 1929–35). Also *Index interpolationum quae in Iustiniani codice inesse dicuntur* (edited by G. Broggini, Weimar, 1969).

Karlowa, *Rechtsgeschichte* 1 and 2

O. Karlowa, *Römische Rechtsgeschichte*, vols. 1 and 2 (Leipzig, 1885–1901).

Kaser, *R.P.R.* 1 and 2

M. Kaser, *Das römische Privatrecht*, vols. 1 and 2 (Munich, 1959) (2nd edition, Munich, 1971).

Lenel, *E.P.*

O. Lenel, *Das Edictum Perpetuum* (3rd edition, Leipzig, 1927).

Lenel, *Pal.* 1 and 2

O. Lenel, *Palingenesia Iuris Civilis*, vols. 1 and 2 (Leipzig, 1889).

Levy, *Vulgar Law*

E. Levy, *West Roman Vulgar Law: The Law of Property* (Philadelphia, 1951).

Nörr, *Die Entstehung*

D. Nörr, *Die Entstehung der longi temporis praescriptio* (Cologne and Opladen, 1969).

O. S. S.	C. E. Otto, B. Schilling, C. F. F. Sintenis, *Das Corpus Iuris Civilis in's Deutsche übersetzt* (Leipzig, 1830–2).
Solazzi, *Specie*	S. Solazzi, *Specie ed estinzione delle servitù prediali* (Naples, 1948).
Solazzi, *Tutela*	S. Solazzi, *La tutela e il possesso delle servitù prediali* (Naples, 1949).
Thesaurus or *T.L.L.*	*Thesaurus linguae latinae* (Leipzig, 1900–).
Vocabularium or *V.I.R.*	*Vocabularium iurisprudentiae romanae* (Berlin, 1900–).
Watson, *Property*	A. Watson, *The Law of Property in the Later Roman Republic* (Oxford, 1969).

For the sake of convenience and brevity, wherever possible references are given to an author's collected papers.

Unless there is an indication to the contrary, the texts referred to are from the Digest.

1. OWNERSHIP

IT is well known that no ancient legal text contains a Roman definition of ownership.[1] However, the belief that owners in Roman law enjoyed virtually unlimited powers over their property, movable or immovable, has an immensely long history and can be said to have influenced all the western legal systems that owe their ultimate allegiance to Roman law. As early as the fourteenth century Bartolus[2] declared that ownership is the *ius de re corporali perfecte disponendi nisi lege prohibeatur* and that notion, so attractively simple and clear-cut, long remained the dominant one: the ideal form of ownership should conform to this pattern.

Thus in the nineteenth century the Pandectists laboured to develop a rigid and sharply defined concept of ownership which corresponded to the intensely individualistic spirit of their age. 'Ownership is as such unlimited; but it suffers limitations', said Windscheid,[3] and when he came to dominate the drafting of what became article 903 of the German Civil Code, his work was inspired by that sentiment.[4] So when the first draft of the Code appeared in 1887, Gierke attacked it generally on the ground that it was too Roman and insufficiently German in character, but specifically he derided its extremely individualistic concept of ownership as an 'uncouth formulation of the Roman concept of ownership'.[5] Its spirit was, he said, that of 'the most rigid Romanism'.[6]

The dispute may have been largely academic, but theoretically Windscheid and Gierke were poles apart and represent two

[1] On ownership in general, see Bonfante, *Corso* 2 1, Chapter 10.
[2] *Opera Omnia* 5 (Venice, 1615 edition), 84. He is discussing 41. 2. 7. 1.
[3] B. Windscheid–T. Kipp, *Lehrbuch des Pandektenrechts* 1 (9th edition, Frankfurt-a.-M., 1906), §167 at 857 ff.
[4] For the drafting of the Code, see in general F. Wieacker, *Privatrechtsgeschichte der Neuzeit* (2nd edition, Göttingen, 1967), 468 ff.
[5] O. von Gierke, *Der Entwurf eines burgerlichen Gesetzbuchs und das deutsche Recht* (revised edition, Leipzig, 1889), 103.
[6] *Der Entwurf*, 323.

different approaches to ownership. For the Pandectists ownership
is in essence unrestricted and any limitations which may be placed
on it are somehow alien to it and detract from its purity, even though,
as Kipp[1] pointed out, there never has been a system of completely
unlimited ownership. Nor, of course, was Windscheid proposing
one. For Gierke, on the other hand, the socially necessary restrictions and controls are of the essence of ownership and are to be
seen not as detracting from it but rather as defining its real nature.
Gierke saw the notion which he preferred in the native German
law and the absolute concept which he despised he called Roman.
In the end, it was Windscheid's concept which reached the statute
book.

Classical Roman Law

   When the Pandectist approach to Roman law was superseded
towards the end of the nineteenth century by that of the modern
historical school, the attitude of scholars to the nature of ownership
did not at first alter dramatically. Instead of attributing absolute
ownership to Roman law, scholars now attributed this ideal concept
to the ideal period of Roman law, the classical period. We even
find the leading Scottish writer on land law declaring proudly that
Scots law has 'preferred to walk in the footsteps of the great
Roman jurists' and to suffer any consequent inconvenience rather
than adopt a system of regulations such as was to be found in
later Roman law.[2] Only gradually did things change. In the 1930s
Schulz wrote, 'The individualistic nature of Roman *ownership*
has often been pointed out, not without some exaggeration.'[3] The
same author warned against attributing to the Romans doctrines
devised by modern Romanistic lawyers,[4] while in an essay first
published during the Second World War Wieacker stresses that
the Pandectists read into the texts what they wished to find there,
a reflection of nineteenth-century individualism.[5]

   [1] Windscheid–Kipp, *Lehrbuch* 1, §167 n. 3 at 857 ff.
   [2] J. Rankine, *The Law of Land-Ownership in Scotland* (4th edition, Edinburgh,
1909), 459 ff.
   [3] F. Schulz, *Principles of Roman Law* (Oxford, 1936), 151. See, however, his
remarks at 153.
   [4] F. Schulz, *Classical Roman Law* (Oxford, 1951), 338.
   [5] See now *Vom Römischen Recht* (2nd edition, Stuttgart, 1961), 187–90 and 220.

When we turn up the relevant pages of a recent textbook, the picture is of anything but the individualistic free-for-all which the older doctrine supposed. Kaser points out that a man had to allow his neighbour to come and collect fruit which had fallen from his tree on to the adjoining land; perhaps even in classical law a man had to tolerate his neighbour's wall projecting half a foot into his land; a right of passage was enforced in an administrative fashion and had to be given by an owner to someone who could not otherwise reach the road; there was a right of way over someone else's land to a (lawful) *sepulchrum*; and a man had to suffer smoke and water coming from his neighbour's land provided it did not exceed the normal amount. On the other hand no one needed to suffer branches of his neighbour's tree overhanging his land and various provisions about removing them were made.[1] The picture given by Jörs and Kunkel[2] is much the same and in each case it is of an ownership hedged about by restrictions which take into account the normal everyday requirements of community living.

The restrictions are not, however, imposed in a uniform fashion. The right of way to an otherwise inaccessible road was always an administrative as opposed to a legal matter; access to a *sepulchrum* on the other hand could be claimed in the provinces at least by *cognitio extraordinaria*.[3] Interdict was the method chosen to protect the right to collect fruit which had fallen into a neighbour's field;[4] two interdicts were used to control overhanging branches.[5] Pomponius,[6] however, reports that the Twelve Tables provided an action to deal with the case of a tree which had been bent by the wind and which now hung over a neighbour's land. A civil-law *actio negatoria* was also available to deal with a neighbour who both sent an excessive amount of water or smoke on to the plaintiff's land and claimed the right to send that amount,[7] while in cases of mere infringement where no right was claimed, the interdict *uti*

---

[1] Kaser, *R.P.R.* 1, 407.
[2] *Römisches Privatrecht* (3rd edition, Berlin, Göttingen, and Heidelberg, 1949), 124.
[3] 11. 7. 12 pr., Ulpian 25 *ad edictum*.
[4] 43. 28. 1 pr., Ulpian 71 *ad edictum*.
[5] 43. 27. 1 pr., Ulpian 71 *ad edictum*; 43. 27. 1. 7, Ulpian 71 *ad edictum*.
[6] 43. 27. 2, Pomponius 34 [33—Lenel] *ad Sabinum*.
[7] 8. 5. 8. 5, Ulpian 17 *ad edictum*. On the text, see below 163 ff.

possidetis may have been available even in classical law.[1] The
ancient *actio aquae pluviae arcendae* lay where rain water had been
diverted by a neighbour and damaged or threatened to damage the
plaintiff's fields. However, the plaintiff in an *actio negatoria* and in
an *actio aquae pluviae arcendae* could not recover damages for any
loss incurred before *litis contestatio*. If he wished to protect himself
fully, a man would therefore take the precaution of obtaining a
cautio damni infecti from his neighbour to cover the loss inflicted
before *litis contestatio*, and this remedy played a major part in
protecting one neighbour against another.

Approaching the problem in this piecemeal fashion, which is
typical of their work, the Roman jurists reconciled the competing
claims of individual owners to have free use of their property.
It is just because the various restrictions are imposed in so many
different ways and are recorded in so many different parts of the
Digest that we may underestimate their combined effect in ensuring
that an owner observes the minimum requirements of life in a
community.[2]

The traditional teaching on building and lights stands in the
starkest contrast to this picture of an ownership qualified by
necessary restrictions, and it has probably played the chief role in
fostering and maintaining the notion of the crudely individualistic
nature of classical ownership. While the other provisions bear
witness to a sensible spirit of tolerance, the idea of unlimited
freedom to build is the acme of intolerance: unless burdened with a
servitude to prevent him, an owner can construct a building on his
land up to any height he likes, even if the effect is to cut off all the
light from his neighbour's building.[3] We may feel that this extreme
freedom is rather out of place, the cuckoo in the nest. Given the

[1] Beseler, 43 (1922) *ZSS* 421 and *Juristische Miniaturen* (Leipzig, 1929),
97 ff. denies that the interdict covered mere disturbance of possession in
classical law, but most writers suppose that some of the texts have a classical
core. See, for instance, Jörs–Kunkel, *Römisches Privatrecht*, 118 n. 5.

[2] There seems no reason to accept Wieacker's notion that in classical law the
necessary restrictions on an owner were provided by servitudes, *Vom Römischen
Recht*, 193.

[3] See for instance W. W. Buckland, *The Main Institutions of Roman Private
Law* (Cambridge, 1931), 155 and more specifically Biondi, *Cat.* 45 and Solazzi,
Specie, 72.

background of the other measures, we should expect something different. We should suppose that an owner must take some account of his neighbour's position and the neighbour could be called upon to tolerate, as in the case of water and smoke, merely a reasonable infringement of his light. It is the purpose of this book to suggest that this was the classical position.

It is useful to spell out the practical effects of the dominant theory. Apparently its supporters think it causes inconvenience but nothing more. We should remind ourselves that we are dealing with a society where daylight was vital, far more so than it is to the average city dweller of today, for in the ancient world there was no satisfactory system of artificial lighting. The lamps which existed provided at best a dim light and if more was wanted large clusters of them had to be used. The light would be not only dim but unsteady and smoky while doubtless the fumes smelled bad. The system was inefficient and the Romans must have attached enormous importance to their only other source of supply, daylight. The large windows and the design of certain types of house around a *peristylium*, early rising and correspondingly early bed-times, all point to the crucial need for daylight. It was all important just because everyday life could not go on without it, there being no effective substitute for it.

In these circumstances even the simplest application of the dominant doctrine becomes a nightmare. Suppose a man has a small house in Rome worth £1,000 and a neighbour builds up his house in such a way that he cuts off the first man's light. The current doctrine abandons the first man to his fate. The daylight has been cut off from his house which is rendered dark, so that he can see nothing, unless with the aid of one of these lamps. From now on, day in day out, he will have to stumble about unable to do the simplest task without carrying his oil lamp with him. Yet for this 'inconvenience' he receives not a farthing's compensation from his neighbour. If, worn out by the strain and his eyes ruined, he tries to sell the house, he will receive nothing for it—who wants to buy a house which is in eternal night? He has lost his £1,000, but he still has no action. Suppose further that our hero was a cobbler and carried on his trade in his house. With his rooms in darkness, he can hardly continue unless he burns dozens of lamps and so increases his costs with the result that his prices become uncompetitive and his trade falls off. Still he has no right of action. If he then gathers up his goods and moves himself and his trade elsewhere, not only does he receive nothing for being unable to sell his house, but he receives nothing for the cost of removing, nothing for the cost of his new house, and nothing for the weeks or months it takes him to re-establish his trade in a new area. Nor can he do anything to prevent this series of catastrophes in the first place. All this in the name of freedom of ownership!

The example is deliberately over-simplified. Wealthy Romans owned and rented large blocks of flats; in real life a plaintiff would come from a higher social class and the facts of a case could be more complex. It is enough if we take a hint from a text of Gaius, 19. 2. 25. 2.[1] Someone has built up his house and as a result the room of a tenant in a neighbouring house has been darkened. We are told that the landlord is liable to the tenant. Actually the text goes on to say that the tenant can give up his lease. This has been attacked as interpolated, but that can be ignored for the moment.[2] All we need to imagine is a landlord with a large block of flats. Someone builds up next to one side of his block with the result that the rooms there become dark. The tenants give up their leases forthwith or they wait on reduced rents till the end of their term and then leave. The landlord has *n* empty flats and no prospect of ever letting them again. Yet he is, we are told, unable to prevent this unless he had the foresight to arrange a servitude *altius non tollendi*. The law is a blackmailer's charter permitting the unscrupulous neighbour to threaten his victim with economic disaster and so to extort vast sums of money in return for a servitude.

Yet if this were happening, we should expect to hear about it not only in the legal sources, but in the lay literature. The man whose house had been ruined in this way would surely crop up from time to time among the persecuted individuals of Roman life. But his plight is overlooked and, as far as I know, we are told of only one case of blackmail, a case not even generally mentioned by supporters of the dominant theory. It involves that singular figure

[1] See below, 10 ff.   [2] See below, 87 ff., for a more detailed examination.

Clodius at the time of his greatest power in Rome in 58 B.C. when Cicero was in exile. Clodius wanted to buy the house of a senator Quintus Seius Postumus in order to link it with another which he owned and so create a more splendid residence. When Quintus Seius refused to sell, Clodius firstly made repeated threats that he would block his lights—*primo se luminibus eius esse obstructurum minabatur*. To these threats Quintus Seius made the bold, if somewhat unfortunate, reply that as long as he (Quintus) lived the house would never belong to Clodius. Clodius took the hint and openly poisoned him, after which he obtained the house by out-bidding all others who wanted to buy and paying about one and a half times its true worth.[1]

At first sight the passage might be thought to support the dominant view, and indeed Nisbet suggests that Quintus Seius would have needed a servitude *altius non tollendi* to stop Clodius.[2] But it would have taken more than a servitude to stop Clodius in his course, and we might as well deduce from the passage that openly committed murder was perfectly legal as that it was per-mitted freely to block another man's lights. If the dominant view is correct, Clodius' threats must have been commonplace. Even if the censors had intervened in earlier times, they were no longer in action in the classical period and their authority had been much debased even before their demise. They could have supplied no real check.

It may be objected to these examples that they are extreme: blocking of lights would not always be so severe or lead to such dire results. That is so, but it does not alter the matter: as the story of Quintus Seius shows, blocking of lights could be so serious as to be threatened by a blackmailer. Yet these are the test cases, for even if they were only a small percentage of the total, no modern adherent of the dominant doctrine has suggested that classical law allowed any modification even for extreme cases. Rather, any modification is portrayed as the meddling of post-classical writers who thereby contaminated the purity of the classical doctrine enshrining freedom of ownership.

[1] *De domo sua* 44. 115.
[2] R. G. Nisbet, *Cicero De domo sua* (Oxford, 1939), 166 ff.

Evidence for the Traditional View of Classical Law

The orthodox view on lights emerges from this survey as both opposed to what we know about the common-sense approach of the rest of Roman *Nachbarrecht* and as producing extraordinary results in practice. Since none of these effects is mentioned by Roman writers, we may wonder what the evidence is for this universally accepted belief. It comes in some ways as a surprise and in others as no surprise to find that only three texts are regularly cited as proof of its existence: 8. 2. 9, C. 3. 34. 8 and C. 3. 34. 9, to which is sometimes added D. 19. 2. 25. 2.[1] It is on the strength of these that the traditional doctrine stands.

Of them 8. 2. 9 is probably the one on which most reliance is put for the simple reason that it is the only Digest text of the classical period which apparently states the principle in a neat straight-forward fashion.

8. 2. 9 Ulpian (53 ad edictum) cum eo, qui tollendo obscurat aedes, quibus non serviat, nulla competit actio.

Ulpian says that there is no action against a person who, by building higher, blocks a house to which he does not owe a servitude. The probative worth of this text as a general principle for classical law is shattered, however, as soon as we investigate its palingenesia. The text comes from Ulpian 53 *ad edictum* where Ulpian was discussing the edict on *damnum infectum*.[2] The edict provided a

---

[1] See, for example, Bonfante, *Corso* 2 1, 287 n. 3; Riccobono, 21 (1896) *RISG* 393 ff. and *Scritti di diritto romano* 1 (Palermo, 1957), 354 and n. 3. It seems pointless to dredge up further examples. Biondi, *Cat.* 98 adds 8. 2. 15, Ulpian 29 *ad Sabinum* to the supposed proofs, but that text proves nothing to the purpose. *Ind. Itp.* It comes from a discussion of *leges mancipi* in connection with sale. Lenel, *Pal.* 2, 1122 ff. Ulpian's purpose was apparently to contrast the servitudes of light and prospect, but the text as we have it shows many stylistic defects and has at the least undergone drastic formal revision. Cf. Beseler, 66 (1948) *ZSS* 309—who goes too far, however, in rejecting everything—and Solazzi, *Specie*, 76. Biondi presumably relies on *si servitus debeatur* but as Solazzi perceives, on the orthodox view this phrase must be extremely doubtful, given the context of comparing two servitudes. At a pinch if one took particular notice of the *quodcumque* and if one accepted the *si servitus debeatur*, the text might even be some support for the notion that the servitude *luminibus non officiendi* merely supplemented an ordinary right to object. However, that is very questionable, given the state of the text. I can see no reason for objecting to the reference to *operis novi nuntiatio* in particular.

[2] Lenel, *E.P.* 371.

procedure for a man to obtain security from his neighbour whose house was in such a dangerous condition that it threatened to cause damage to the applicant. The neighbour would have to undertake to pay any loss (*damnum*) which the applicant suffered. 8. 2. 9 comes from a discussion of what is to be counted as loss in this context.

Lenel places our text next to 39. 2. 13. 10 which he assigns to the discussion of the words *ei qui iuraverit non calumniae causa id se postulare* in the edict,[1] but he himself says that 8. 2. 9 could perhaps be put elsewhere.[2] In this he was correct, for 8. 2. 9 comes from earlier in Ulpian's commentary where he was commenting on the opening word of the edict, *damni*.[3] No other comment on that word itself has survived in the Digest fragments though there is much on the *infecti* part of *damni infecti*,[4] and there is no reason to think that the idea of *damnum* would not also have been expounded, that part having been cut out by the compilers.

That something like this was the origin of the text is shown by a comparison with 39. 2. 24. 12, Ulpian 81 *ad edictum*, *h.t.* 25, Paul 78 *ad edictum* and *h.t.* 26, Ulpian 81 *ad edictum*. All these texts will require consideration in due course, but at the moment we need only notice that 25 and 26 are concerned at least in part with whether or not blocking of a neighbour's lights can amount to *damnum* within the meaning of that word in the *cautio damni infecti*. Lenel points out that 39. 2. 24. 12 and *h.t.* 26 form part of Ulpian's remarks on that section of the *cautio* which runs *quod . . . damnum factum erit*.[5] Although Lenel[6] does not give a precise situation for 39. 2. 25 beyond its coming from Paul's commentary on the *cautio damni infecti*, it is natural to deduce from comparison with the texts of Ulpian, 39. 2. 24. 12 and *h.t.* 26, that like them it was a comment on the word *damnum*.

At the most Ulpian said that no action for *damnum infectum* would lie against an owner who, while not burdened with a

---

[1] *Pal.* 2, 748 n. 3. [2] *Pal.* 2, 748 n. 4.

[3] *Damni* is the opening word in Lenel's version. See, however, *E.P.* 372 n. 1.

[4] See *Pal.* 2, Ulpian no. 1272.

[5] *Pal.* 2, 883 n. 3. Curiously enough he refrains from assigning a context to either in his *E.P.* 552 n. 4 though 39. 2. 24. 12 self-evidently deals with what amounts to *damnum*. In an earlier note he seems to bracket 24. 12 and *h.t.* 26 with 24. 2–11. *E.P.* 551 n. 7. [6] *Pal.* 1, 1095.

servitude, raised his house and so blocked his neighbour's lights. Ulpian's statement was limited to the scope of the action on *damnum infectum* but the compilers have cut it out from its context and have given it a new and extended meaning: what was once a remark about *damnum infectum* is now a cornerstone of the law of servitudes. They may have done nothing except move the text to its new home, but it is likely that their generalization was more radical and that at the very least the clause *quibus non serviat*, in which the subjunctive is unharmonious, represents, as Solazzi thought,[1] an addition by them to make the text fit better into its new home.

This method of generalization is a well-known phenomenon and Professor Daube has made a penetrating study of all its aspects.[2] What emerges is that the compilers may make such generalizations either because they cannot find a neat statement of the classical principle within the *sedes materiae* or else because they are changing to a new principle which they cannot find in the classical material but to which they lend an air of respectability by fabricating it in this way out of classical material.[3] Solazzi would tend to the first view of the case which now lies before us: for him the principle in the text is so obvious that Ulpian would not have needed to state it.[4] However, it would be possible to say on the basis of this text that no such principle existed and that it was a mere creation of the compilers. The text is no help for the traditional theory which it is said to support and there is thus no explicit statement in its favour in the Digest.

For convenience we now take the other Digest text which is sometimes cited. It is quickly disposed of since it provides no support for the traditional theory.

19. 2. 25. 2 Gaius (10 ad edictum provinciale) si vicino aedificante obscurentur lumina cenaculi, teneri locatorem inquilino: certe quin liceat colono vel inquilino relinquere conductionem, nulla dubitatio est.

---

[1] *Specie*, 105 n. 252. He went too far in suspecting the whole text. *Tutela*, 163 ff. Perhaps he was right to suspect the construction with the owner, not the property as the subject of *servire* though this would require due investigation.

[2] Daube, 76 (1959) *ZSS* 149.

[3] For this second procedure, see especially Daube, 76 *ZSS* 237–44.

[4] *Tutela*, 164.

de mercedibus quoque si cum eo agatur, reputationis ratio habenda est. eadem intellegemus, si ostia fenestrasve nimium corruptas locator non restituat.

The text tells us that if a neighbour builds and blocks the lights of a room which has been let, the landlord is liable to the tenant. The text then goes on to discuss the form of that liability. We can reconcile this with any system: the landlord may be liable to the tenant even though the neighbour was free to build and he could not prevent him; equally—or one might think *a fortiori*—the landlord may be liable to the tenant in a system where the neighbour is not free to build and could have been prevented.

The Code texts are both constitutions of Diocletian from the year A.D. 293. In date they are post-classical, but Diocletian's chancellery is widely credited with making attempts to keep the law as classical as possible.

C. 3. 34. 8 [*Impp. Diocletianus et Maximianus*] *A.A. et C.C. Aniceto.* altius quidem aedificia tollere, si domus servitutem non debeat, dominus eius minime prohibetur. in pariete vero tuo si fenestram Iulianus vi vel clam fecisse convincatur, sumptibus suis opus tollere et integrum parietem restituere compellitur. [a. 293]

The part which is generally quoted in this field is the first sentence which says that if a house does not owe a servitude, then its owner is not prevented at all from raising the buildings.

It can be said immediately that this first part of the text was originally somewhat different. As we have it now, it contains merely a succinct statement of principle while the details about the circumstances of the decision have been cut out. This much is clear even from the *vero* in the second sentence for, as Solazzi remarked,[1] that indicates some kind of connection between the case in the second sentence and the case in the first sentence, while, as the text stands at present, the one has little obvious bearing on the other. The names of the parties have also vanished from this first part and Iulianus does not appear till the second sentence.

This being so, the value of the text as a statement of principle on which to found a theory about classical law is reduced. We can detect the hand of the compilers pruning away the surrounding

[1] *Specie*, 87.

context and without that context it is not possible to gauge the scope of the principle. They may have made changes in substance but even assuming that the text said something like what it says now, we could imagine situations of which a statement such as this might be written in a system which allowed an owner to object if his neighbour severely blocked his lights—for example, it could apply where the effect of the blocking did not exceed the reasonably tolerable. Torn from such a context it would perform its present role. This sentence taken by itself does not amount to sufficient proof of the principle in classical law.

What follows is an attempt to go a step further and try to suggest what the first part of the text may have said before the compilers set to work on it, but the main result is to reveal how difficult it would be to reconstruct the original substance.

The second half of the text is rather more informative than the first and tells us: 'But if Julian is proved to have made a window *vi* or *clam* in your wall, then he is compelled to remove the work and restore the wall to its original state at his own cost.' Solazzi complains that *vi vel clam* is objectionable, because the plaintiff Anicetus would accuse the defendant of acting in one way or the other, while if the point was taken by the emperor he should have included *precario* also. This last objection is unsound, if we suppose that the remedy which Anicetus is seeking is the interdict *quod vi aut clam*,[1] and even the first is not particularly strong since we do not know the facts: there could be elements of both.[2] Alternatively it could just be a full reference to the interdict called *vi aut clam*. The important matter is identifying the remedy as the interdict and there seems nothing against it: *opus*, *tollere*, and *restituere* are all words which fit into the area of discussion of this interdict,[3] since its purpose was to make the defendant remove structures put up *vi* or *clam* and restore the plaintiff to the position in which he was before the building was begun. Furthermore, the situation envisaged could be seen as a possible case for decision, the question in issue being whether or not knocking out a

---

[1] Already suggested by the Gloss, *Altius, ad h.t.*
[2] Cf. 43. 24. 11. 5, Ulpian 71 *ad edictum.*
[3] Cf. merely 43. 24. 21 pr., Pomponius 29 *ad Sabinum.*

window in someone's wall amounted to a work *in solo* such as was required in practice though not by the wording of the edict.[1] The answer was that this did fall within the scope of the interdict, a reasonable decision which would be in line with others of which we know.[2]

It is a fair assumption that the different parts of any imperial constitution are in some way related to one another. In our case that presumption is raised to virtual certainty by the particle *vero* in the second sentence. It has an adversative force, contrasting the two sentences and presumably indicating that while the plaintiff was successful in the second half of the constitution his first plea failed. We have seen that it is reasonable to suppose that the second sentence is about the interdict *quod vi aut clam* and it is therefore not altogether far-fetched to suggest that the first sentence may also be about that interdict so that whereas it was to be granted in the second case it was to be denied in the first. Slightly in favour of our supposition of the interdict in this first part is the use of the word *prohibetur* there: it is a technical term in connection with this interdict, though it is usually used absolutely and not with a dependent infinitive.[3] If we were to take the clause in this way, it would say that if a house does not owe a servitude, its owner is not at all prevented (by the interdict *quod vi aut clam*) from raising the buildings.

Taken just like this, as it stands, the clause would not make sense in the context of the interdict, since according to what we are told elsewhere, the question of the defendant's right to do the work is not judged in this interdict: the interdict lies because of the way the work is done.[4] Hence it should not make any difference whether or not Anicetus has a servitude. If then the text did originally have something to do with the interdict, we should have to say that the reference to the servitude was in some way false. If it is deleted, then the text suggests a reply to a problem on the interdict: the interdict will not lie against an owner who builds up his house,

---

[1] See, for example, 43. 24. 7. 5, Ulpian 71 *ad edictum.*

[2] *arg.* 43. 24. 22. 2, Venuleius 2 *interdictorum.*

[3] See H. G. Heumann–E. Seckel, *Handlexicon zu den Quellen des römischen Rechts* (9th edition, Jena, 1907), s.v. *prohibere.*

[4] 43. 24. 1. 2, Ulpian 71 *ad edictum.*

because it does not lie against someone who acts *in suo*. This principle seems to have been the classical one, as Bonfante argues,[1] though the matter is not beyond doubt. The clearest statement is in 39. 1. 5. 10, Ulpian 52 *ad edictum*. By saying that *operis novi nuntiatio* is necessary where the work is done *in suo*, this implies that an interdict *quod vi aut clam* is not competent. In the text under notice Anicetus would have put two problems: firstly would the interdict *quod vi aut clam* lie where Iulianus had built his house up and blocked Anicetus' lights, and secondly would it lie where Iulianus had made a window in Anicetus' wall? The answers would be: the interdict would not lie in the first case because an owner cannot be prevented in this way from raising his house, but if on the other hand it is a question of your wall and Iulianus has made a window in it, then the interdict will lie.

This is all extremely speculative and would mean that the first sentence of C. 3. 34. 8 has been rewritten by the compilers to give a neat statement of the freedom-to-build principle. On the traditional view that idea is out of the question because the compilers are working on the opposite principle, but that objection is of no force since we have seen them deliberately frame the freedom principle in 8. 2. 9. We can be certain that, whatever stood at the start of C. 3. 34. 8 when written by Diocletian's jurists, the compilers have taken care to form the succinct statement of principle which we find there now. The feeling must grow that, contrary to the common view, the compilers were in favour of this freedom-to-build doctrine.

C. 3. 34. 9 is an even harder text.

[*Impp. Diocletianus et Maximianus*] *A.A. et C.C. Zosimo*. si in aedibus vicini tibi debita servitute parietem altius aedificavit Heraclius, novum opus suis sumptibus per praesidem provinciae tollere compellitur. sed si te servitutem habuisse non probetur, tollendi altius aedificium vicino non est interdictum. [a. 293]

The last sentence is the piece which is generally quoted and the rest of the constitution is ignored. The German translation renders it: 'Aber wenn nicht bewiesen wird, dass du eine Dienstbarkeit

---

[1] *Corso* 2 1, 416 ff. The doubts are caused by 8. 5. 6. 1, Ulpian 17 *ad edictum* and 7. 4. 5. 3, Ulpian 17 *ad Sabinum* with 7. 4. 6, Pomponius 5 *ad Sabinum*.

gehabt habest, so ist es dem Nachbar nicht untersagt, sein Haus
höher zu bauen.'[1] Biondi[2] cites it for the proposition that 'the
owner can build *unlimitedly*, as long as that power is not restricted
by an appropriate servitude (a voluntary one)'. For Solazzi[3] it
shows that 'the owner immune from any "passive" servitudes, has
every power over his own thing'. From this it would appear that
these writers would take the last sentence in the same way as the
German version, and would wish to translate it 'But if it is not
proved that you have a servitude, your neighbour is not forbidden
to raise his building higher.'

The overwhelming belief in the traditional view coupled with
scholars' comparative lack of interest in the Code explains why this
text survived the wildest excesses of radical interpolationism so
that no hint of a doubt was raised until as late as 1951 when
Solazzi drew attention to grave deficiencies.[4] Firstly, he notes
that the constitution really says the same thing twice over: if there
is a servitude, Zosimus can force Heraclius to remove the offending
portion, and then if there is not, Zosimus cannot force him. Such
repetition is not to be expected from Diocletian. Secondly, says
Solazzi, *probetur* is odd because Zosimus ought to prove the
existence of the servitude; *probes* would be better. Thirdly, the
perfect tense *habuisse* is unjustified because the servitude has not
ceased to exist. Fourthly, the *vicinus* and Heraclius are one and the
same so that the text should have read *in aedibus Heraclii . . . is
parietem altius aedificavit.*

Not all of these objections are to be accepted. The first objection
is sound: the later part of the constitution is banal and adds nothing
which would not be obvious from what goes before. As long as we
assume that the action in question is the *actio confessoria*, Solazzi's
objection to *probetur* is justified though perhaps not too serious.
The objection to *habuisse* is warranted and it is hard to see how
that tense can be defended. The fourth objection is wide of the

---

[1] O. S. S. 5, 496.   [2] *Cat.* 45.   [3] *Specie*, 72.
[4] 2 (1951) *IURA* 13 ff. Psychologically it is fascinating to notice that Solazzi
saw these difficulties when he was concerned with a marginal point of terminology, but remained, as far as we know, blind to them when dealing with the
central problem of the *ius altius tollendi* in his book *Specie*. Nothing could better
illustrate the hold of the orthodox view.

mark. Although, for example, the Gloss and Otto–Schilling–Sintenis also[1] amalgamate the personalities of the *vicinus* and Heraclius, there is no justification for doing so. Call the neighbour X. The situation envisaged is where Heraclius (who is perhaps a tenant) raises X's house and blocks Zosimus' lights. The constitution says that Heraclius must remove the addition at his own cost.

We can add an even more serious formal objection, which goes to the heart of the second sentence. Given the proximity of C. 3. 34. 8 which has a statement to a similar effect, the traditional view probably represents what the text in its present form is meant to say. None the less, the Latin is impossible. To achieve the traditional translation we must take *tollendi . . . non est interdictum* as 'it is not forbidden . . . to raise', but no rule of Latin grammar will permit *interdicere* to be followed by a gerund. A Roman jurist might write *interdicere* with an infinitive, or *interdicere ne*, or even *interdicere ut*, but never *interdicere* with a gerund. To add to the confusion, the gerund is in the genitive case. There seems to be no parallel for this usage[2] and it simply will not do.

If a solution is sought in construing *interdictum* as a noun (and this has never been done), the literal translation would have to be something like 'There is no ban on (interdict against) the neighbour raising the building'. This is not only artificial but involves giving the meaning 'on' or 'against' to the dative *vicino* depending on the noun *interdictum*. Although *interdicere* with the dative is usual and correct for 'to prohibit someone', the noun *interdictum* with a dative is not possible: the usual construction would be with a preposition such as *adversus*. Taking *interdictum* as a noun then leads to equally great grammatical difficulties.[3] The slightly older manuscript P reads *vicini*, which may have been the original reading. It is certainly at first sight *difficilior* and a scribe despairing of making sense of the passage would eagerly correct to *vicino*. All the same the impression is strong that the text in its present form was meant to read as a statement of freedom to build.

---

[1] Gloss *si in aedibus*. O. S. S. 5, 496.

[2] See *T.L.L.* 7 1, 2173–5. The *Thesaurus* maintains a discreet silence about our text.

[3] I leave out of account as unrealistic any translation based on *vicino* as a dative of agent depending on *tollendi*.

A further small point is the use of the verb *tollere*. This occurs twice in the text, in the first sentence with the meaning 'to remove' and in the second sentence with its other meaning 'to raise'. This is inelegant and one may surmise that the writer of the first sentence avoided just this awkwardness when he chose to write *altius aedificavit*. The same inelegance occurs in C. 3. 34. 8, the immediately preceding text.[1]

Formally the crucial sentence of this constitution could not be worse, and we can have no hesitation in saying that it is not what Diocletian wrote. The trend nowadays is to distrust formal indications as pointers to a change in substance, but we may recall that Solazzi pointed out that the second sentence adds nothing. In these circumstances we are not guilty of any grave excess of radicalism in choosing to believe that the relevant sentence may also be interpolated as to substance.

After a great deal of thought I despair of suggesting what the second sentence may have said. It may indeed be a complete fabrication of the compilers to stress the principle of freedom to build. The first sentence is not explicit, but the verbs *tollere compellitur* might lead one to suppose that the remedy in question is an interdict—as also might the word *opus* which is common in such contexts, *opus novum* indeed being not altogether unknown.[2] The supposition of an interdict might be backed up by the rather curious fact situation involving Heraclius, the neighbour, and Zosimus. In the normal case, where an owner acts *in suo* the interdict *quod vi aut clam* does not, as we saw, operate, but it would operate in just such a case as this if Heraclius were perhaps a tenant and built on X's land.[3]

The word *interdictum* in the last sentence, judging by the gerund dependent on it, might be a noun and could therefore be taken in its technical sense of an interdict. However, that supposition brings fresh problems. Firstly, if the interdict is *quod vi aut clam* there must have been either a *prohibitio* or some clandestine

---

[1] Cf. also the (different) confusion of meanings in a constitution of Justinian, C. 8. 51 (52). 3 pr., i.e. C. 1. 4. 24.

[2] 43. 24. 6, Paul 67 *ad edictum*.

[3] See for instance 39. 3. 4. 2 and 3, Ulpian 53 *ad edictum*. Bonfante, *Corso* 2 1, 409 ff.

element which does not feature in the present text. This might be allowed—there has doubtless been abbreviation. Then taking a most literal rendering of the second sentence, one could say that it meant 'But if it is not proved you had a servitude, there is no interdict to remove the higher structure of your neighbour' (reading *vicini*). Leaving aside the tortured and controversial elements in the rendering, does it make legal sense? The answer seems to be No, for it would mean that Zosimus' title to the interdict was dependent on proving that he had a servitude. That is intolerable, because Zosimus is awarded the interdict on account of the nature of Heraclius' operations and the question of whether or not Zosimus has a servitude does not enter into the matter. That must await a separate action about the servitude.

Any solution based on translating *vicino non est interdictum* as 'the neighbour has no interdict' suffers at the outset from the major drawback that we should not expect a rescript addressed to Zosimus to be concerned with whether or not the neighbour is entitled to an interdict. Besides, if Heraclius built on X's land and that building was *vi* or *clam*, X would have a right to the interdict whether or not Zosimus had a servitude.

One could perhaps suggest other permutations but the chances of detecting a sensible meaning beneath the surface of the second sentence are remote. It is at best an adaptation of some old part of the constitution which we can no longer reconstruct, but it may be a complete invention of the compilers. They may have misunderstood the purport of the first sentence or have deliberately misinterpreted it so that by drawing a distinction between the situation with and without a servitude, they could formulate a neat principle. We need not try too hard to see what the constitution originally said, since all that matters for our task is that the second sentence shows every sign of being spurious.

The result of this section is simple. Three texts are regularly cited for the principle of unrestricted freedom to build. They are 8. 2. 9, C. 3. 34. 8 and C. 3. 34. 9. The first has been generalized by the compilers and originally referred exclusively to *damnum infectum*. The second has also been generalized by the compilers and the original context of the statement is lost. The relevant

sentence of C. 3. 34. 9 is formally so disgraceful as to leave no doubt
that it is not what Diocletian wrote. This means that the principal
texts which are cited to support the freedom to build doctrine are
the flimsiest possible evidence for classical law. Accepting this, we
are free to look at the problem of building and lights in classical
law from a new standpoint. In other words, leaving behind these
three supposed guides, we may reconstruct the classical position
from the rest of the texts.

By far the most important matter for re-examination is the
servitude *altius tollendi*. At first sight, one would expect that a
servitude with this name would give the dominant owner the right
to raise his building, just as the opposite servitude *altius non
tollendi* unquestionably gives the dominant owner the right to
prevent the servient owner from raising a building on the servient
land. Yet such an explanation has had to be abandoned, simply
because it has been assumed that unless there was a servitude
altius non tollendi to prevent him, an owner, merely by virtue of
being owner, was free to build as high as he liked. There would
therefore be no room for a servitude to bestow the right to build
and some other meaning for the servitude *altius tollendi* has had to
be found. The weaknesses of the theories concocted to provide this
other meaning have always been apparent to all except their
advocates and they need not be investigated here.[1]

Now that the supposed proofs of this extreme freedom to build
in classical law have been seen to be worthless, the servitude *altius
tollendi* can be given the straightforward meaning which brings it
into line with the servitude *altius non tollendi*. However, since the
very existence of the servitude *altius tollendi* in classical law has
been challenged, it is necessary first to examine the texts which
mention the *ius altius tollendi* to see whether they are genuine.

Evidence for the Servitude Altius Tollendi *in Classical Law*

Quite a few passages must be examined in deciding whether the
classical law included this servitude. An important part of the
evidence is formed by texts containing lists of servitudes, some

---

[1] For the older writers, see D. C. F. Glück, *Ausführliche Erläuterung* 10 1
(Erlangen, 1808), 77 ff. For modern views, Grosso, *Servitù*, 237 n. 6.

mentioning the servitude *altius tollendi*, others not.[1] Besides these
texts containing lists, there are others which mention several servitudes and again the significance of a writer referring to the servitude
or omitting it must be assessed.[2] C. 3. 34. 1 and D. 8. 5. 6. 1 also
argue in favour of the existence of a servitude *altius tollendi*.[3]
After the rest of the evidence has been scrutinized in this way,
two texts (G. 4. 3 and J. 4. 6. 2) which are commonly thought to
talk about a servitude *altius tollendi*, but which do not, must be
explained.[4] We start, however, with the texts which give lists of
servitudes.

Chronologically, the first text is 8. 3. 2 pr.:

> Neratius (4 regularum) rusticorum praediorum servitutes sunt
> licere altius tollere et officere praetorio vicini, vel cloacam habere licere
> per vicini domum vel praetorium, vel protectum habere licere.

This passage is awkward from another point of view, because it
lists three apparently typical urban servitudes and calls them
rustic. No satisfactory solution to this riddle has been proposed,[5]
but that aspect of the text may be left on one side, since *pace*
Grosso[6] it is not obvious that there would be any connection
between this odd classification and the part which concerns us,
talk of a servitude *altius tollendi*.

Solazzi[7] thinks that the servitude should be *altius non tollendi*.
Apart from general allusions to the problem just mentioned, his
only clear objection to the form is that *servitutes sunt licere . . .* is
detestable Latin. This criticism appears unduly harsh: a predicative
use of the infinitive is common enough with certain nouns in
Republican Latin and this usage was extended to other nouns in
later writers.[8] Having made this none too forceful objection Solazzi
merely claims that he has reached the point in his researches where
he can say that a text mentioning only the servitude *altius tollendi*
and not the servitude *altius non tollendi* 'which we ought to think of
as the more common and important' cannot be genuine. We have

---

[1] Below, 20 ff.   [2] Below, 25 ff.   [3] Below, 28 ff.
[4] Below, 30 ff.   [5] Solazzi, *Specie*, 5 ff. and refs.
[6] *Studi in memoria di Aldo Albertoni* 1 (Padua, 1935), 466.
[7] *Specie*, 96 ff.
[8] M. Leumann–J. B. Hofmann–A. Szantyr, *Lateinische Grammatik* 2 (Munich, 1955), 349².

not reached that happy position and so this reason has no validity
for us. The question of the relative frequency and importance of
the servitudes will receive attention below.

In fact the positive form fits the text well since the two other
servitudes mentioned and introduced as alternatives by *vel* are
also positive. A negative servitude would be slightly out of place in
this list and there would have to be strong reasons to compel us to
insert *non* which would spoil the symmetry of the text.

The next authority, and the most important, is Gaius.

G. 2. 14 . . . eodem numero sunt iura praediorum urbanorum et
rustico*rum*. praedio*rum urbanorum iura sunt velut ius* altius tollendi
aedes et officiendi luminibus vicini aed*ium aut* non extollendi, ne
luminibus vicini officiatur, item fluminum et stillicidiorum *ius, id est ut
vicinus flumen vel stillicidium* in aream *vel in aedes suas recipiat; item
cloacae immittendae et luminum immittendorum* . . .

All the words, and parts of words, in italics are conjectural and
are a reconstruction by Krüger[1] on the basis of G. Ep. 2. 1. 3 and
D. 8. 2. 2. David and Nelson think that the reconstruction of the
first part is satisfactory.[2] Important words for us, *altius tollendi*,
are legible. They raise a strong presumption that Gaius referred
here to the *ius altius tollendi*. In theory, a *non* could have stood
before the *altius*, but this is unlikely since a sound piece of text
slightly further on mentions the negative form of the servitude.
Especially when the text is read against the background of
D. 8. 2. 2, this makes it more likely than not that Gaius here spoke
of the positive servitude.[3] This assertion is essentially independent
of any purely conjectural part of the text and so is not struck at by
Solazzi when he refuses to accept the popular reconstruction.[4]
What Solazzi means when he rejects the reconstruction is to argue
that even if it accurately reflects what the Verona Manuscript would
have contained had it been legible at this point, none the less the
text is not what Gaius himself wrote: it is a gloss, and a gloss by the

---

[1] Cf. E. Seckel and B. Kübler, *Gai Institutiones* (8th edition, Leipzig, 1939),
ad loc.

[2] *Gai Institutionum. Kommentar* (Leiden, 1960), 240 ff.

[3] So Grosso, *Studi Albertoni* 1, 467 ff.

[4] *Specie*, 92 ff.

same person who glossed G. 2. 31 and to same effect.[1] Since there is nothing in the text itself which justifies that attitude it must be founded on *a priori* grounds. These will be looked at later; all that matters for our present purposes is that we have a text which, looked at by itself, suggests that Gaius knew of a servitude *altius tollendi*. Still, the text is not in good condition and for that reason no one has relied on it, modern writers preferring to concentrate on G. 2. 31:

sed haec scilicet in Italicis praediis ita sunt, quia et ipsa praedia mancipationem et in iure cessionem recipiunt. alioquin in provincialibus praediis sive quis usumfructum sive ius eundi agendi aquamve ducendi vel altius tollendi aedes aut non tollendi, ne luminibus vicini officiatur, ceteraque similia iura constituere velit, pactionibus et stipulationibus id efficere potest; quia ne ipsa quidem praedia mancipationem aut in iure cessionem recipiunt.

Solazzi[2] would delete as glosses *vel altius tollendi–similia iura* and *quia ne ipsa–recipiunt*. We need not concern ourselves with the latter part, which, even if a gloss, would be harmless. The first part is more important. Solazzi says that *aut non tollendi, ne luminibus vicini officiatur* confuses two distinct types of servitude, presumably *altius non tollendi* and *ne luminibus officiatur*. This is hardly so: the words *ne luminibus vicini officiatur* serve rather to define in a fairly sophisticated way the scope of the servitude *altius non tollendi* which may originally have been rather more crudely formulated. The fact that no other servitude in the list is so defined does not speak against the genuineness of the clause for none of the others requires such definition. In fact Solazzi later withdrew his objection to this part.[3] He takes exception to *aut* after *vel* and *sive*. *Sive* has little to do with the matter; it is being used to separate off usufruct from the praedial servitudes: *sive quis usumfructum sive ius eundi . . . constituere velit*. *Vel* on the other hand serves to mark off the rustic from the urban servitudes. Within that class of urban servitudes Gaius then introduces an alternative of raising or not raising a house and for this he uses *aut*.

---

[1] Glosse a Gaio 2 (II 5–146), *Per Il XIV Centenario della Codificazione Guistinianea* (Pavia, 1934), 347 ff.

[2] Glosse a Gaio 2, 344 ff.   [3] *Specie*, 91 n. 208.

There is nothing wrong with that and no question of a clash with *sive* or *vel* arises. Gaius uses *aut* in the same position in D. 8. 2. 2. These objections of Solazzi are groundless. He later[1] added to them, but to little effect, as Branca has demonstrated.[2] For example, Solazzi said that *ne luminibus vicini officiatur* was the complement of both the *ius altius tollendi aedes* and the *ius altius non tollendi* whereas it should apply to the second only. Branca quite rightly replied that the natural way to read the text was by taking *ne luminibus . . .* with what comes just before, and that to insist on construing it with *altius tollendi* is simply to create an objection which does not exist. For the remainder, it is sufficient to refer to Branca's study while noting that we shall come back later to Solazzi's objection that the positive form is mentioned before the negative form, a complaint similar to the one which we saw him making in connection with 8. 3. 2 pr.[3]

If we look at the text in isolation and without feeling in advance that any mention of a *ius altius tollendi* is inherently absurd, G. 2. 31 provides further evidence for its existence. Still more evidence is provided by 8. 2. 2, Gaius 7 *ad edictum provinciale*:

urbanorum praediorum iura talia sunt: altius tollendi et officiendi luminibus vicini aut non extollendi item stillicidium avertendi in tectum vel aream vicini aut non avertendi: item immittendi tigna in parietem vicini et denique proiciendi protegendive ceteraque istis similia.

Solazzi gives four reasons for holding our part interpolated.[4] Firstly, it is incompatible with the certain principle that a man could block his neighbour's lights. Since there is no trustworthy evidence of such a principle in classical law, this objection need not detain us. Secondly, G. 2. 31 is glossed and hence 8. 2. 2 which contains the same doctrine must be unsound also. If Solazzi's proof of the gloss in G. 2. 31 is not accepted this reasoning is not persuasive. Thirdly 'for the traditional and constant teaching of the classical jurists': from J. 2. 3. 1 it seems that Ulpian did not mention the servitude *altius tollendi* in his list. In fact that is the only list in which it does not feature. Fourthly, the words *et officiendi luminibus vicini* are both useless and dangerous. Apparently the danger is

---

[1] *Specie*, 90 ff.   [2] *Studi in onore di Cicu* 1 (Milan, 1951), 107 ff.
[3] See below, 33 ff.; also above, 20 ff.   [4] *Specie*, 93 ff.

that people would reason thus on account of the parallel phrasing of the servitudes: the servitude *altius non tollendi* prohibits building higher which blocks lights and allows that which does not block lights; therefore the servitude *altius tollendi et officiendi* must allow building which blocks lights and prohibit building which does not block lights. As Solazzi says, this is sophistry. It is also grotesque and no counter-argument is required.

G. Ep. 2. 1. 3 can also be associated with the name of Gaius:

incorporalia etiam sunt iura praediorum urbanorum vel rusticorum praediorum urbanorum iura sunt stillicidia, fenestrae, cloacae, altius erigendae domus aut non erigendae et luminum, ut ita quis fabricet, ut vicinae domui lumen non tollat.

Not too much weight can be given to this text, at least as authority for classical law. The Epitome is unreliable, the section on servitudes being particularly confused.[1] The text does indicate that the writer meant to refer to a servitude *altius tollendi*, however he may have understood the term. Since the passage ultimately derives from something to do with Gaius' Institutes—presumably G. 2. 14—it confirms the impression already formed that Gaius referred to a *ius altius tollendi*.

The last text which gives this kind of list is J. 2. 3. 1 which almost certainly comes from Ulpian's institutes.[2]

praediorum urbanorum sunt servitutes, quae aedificiis inhaerent, ideo urbanorum praediorum dictae, quoniam aedificia omnia urbana praedia appellantur, etsi in villa aedificata sunt. item praediorum urbanorum servitutes sunt hae: ut vicinus onera vicini sustineat: ut in parietem eius liceat vicino tignum immittere: ut stillicidium vel flumen recipiat quis in aedes suas vel in aream, vel non recipiat: et ne altius tollat quis aedes suas, ne luminibus vicini officiatur.

Solazzi thinks that the fact that Ulpian does not mention the servitude *altius tollendi* proves that it did not exist at this time. However, as we have noted, this is the only list which does not mention the positive form. We cannot avoid the difficulty by saying that Ulpian is listing servitudes from the point of view of

---

[1] In general, F. Schulz, *Roman Legal Science* (corrected edition, Oxford, 1953), 302–4. In particular, G. G. Archi, *L' "Epitome Gai" Studio sul tardo diritto romano in occidente* (Milan, 1937), 230–5.

[2] C. Ferrini, *Opere* 2 (Milan, 1929), 360.

burdens on the servient owner, since the *altius tollendi* could have been introduced as allowing a neighbour to build and block your lights. What makes the omission even more curious and tantalizing is that while this list is the only one to omit the servitude *altius tollendi*, it is one of only two lists which mention the supposedly enigmatic servitude *stillicidii non recipiendi*. The text is odd also in another not unrelated way. The servitudes appear in their correct edictal order except for the servitude *altius non tollendi* which comes last in the list when it would be expected to precede the others.[1] It may be that the author had didactic reasons for separating this negative servitude from the positive ones, but we cannot know.

We have exhausted the texts giving lists of servitudes in one connection or another. There are other texts in which a number are mentioned. Firstly another text of Gaius.

8. 4. 16 (2 rerum cottidianarum) potest etiam in testamento heredem suum quis damnare, ne altius aedes suas tollat, ne luminibus aedium vicinarum officiat, vel ut patiatur eum tignum in parietem immittere, vel stillicidia adversus eum habere, vel ut patiatur vicinum per fundum suum vel heredis ire agere aquamve ex eo ducere.

The text with variations appears also as J. 2. 3. 4.

si quis velit vicino aliquod ius constituere pactionibus atque stipulationibus id efficere debet. potest etiam in testamento quis heredem suum damnare, ne altius tollat, ne luminibus aedium vicini officiat: vel ut patiatur eum tignum in parietem immittere vel stillicidium habere: vel ut patiatur eum per fundum ire agere aquamve ex eo ducere.

For the sake of the argument and because the passage in Justinian's Institutes relates to servitudes in the law of his time, I propose to deal with it on that basis. At the same time, it may be pointed out that there is no mention of servitudes in 8. 4. 16 and only the context in the Digest suggests that Gaius is definitely talking about them. The text is explicable on the supposition that the arrangements in question are merely legacies and not legacies of servitudes.[2] In that case the texts could be ignored as evidence for

---

[1] For the order, see Lenel, *E.P.* 194.
[2] The palingenesia of 8. 4. 16 need not be against this. Lenel puts the text under *De servitutibus. Pal.* 1, 257. Possible, of course—and even just possible if it relates to legacies. It is widely held that the author of the *res cottidianae* did not

servitudes in classical law. But if they are treated as servitude texts, then Gaius is discussing various burdens which a testator can place as servitudes over his heir's land. Among them he lists the servitude *altius non tollendi*, but not the servitude *altius tollendi*. It is clear that, if such a servitude existed, Gaius *could* have mentioned a servitude *altius tollendi* which would give a neighbour the right to build and block the heir's lights. It is doubtful none the less if much importance should be attached to the fact that Gaius does not mention the servitude *altius tollendi*. Since Gaius does not claim to be giving a complete list, he would be at liberty not to mention the servitude *altius tollendi* even though it existed and could be appropriate in the context.

In 8. 2. 1 pr., Paul apparently does mention the *ius altius tollendi*.

Paul (21 ad edictum) si intercedat solum publicum vel via publica, neque itineris actusve neque altius tollendi servitutes impedit: sed immittendi protegendi prohibendi, item fluminum et stillicidiorum servitutem impedit, quia caelum, quod supra id solum intercedit, liberum esse debet.

Paul's discussion has undergone revision and amalgamation.[1] Grosso says that a *non* has probably fallen out between *altius* and *tollendi*.[2] His principal argument is that the present text comes from the same book as 8. 3. 7. 1 and 8. 5. 5, in the second of which Paul says that a servitude *altius non tollendi* can be imposed on a house which is separated by another from the dominant tenement. From that Grosso deduces that 8. 2. 1 pr. probably also referred to the servitude *altius non tollendi*. The argument is of little force. For one thing, Paul was aware that this kind of question could arise in relation to the servitude *altius tollendi* because he discusses it in 8. 4. 7. 1, Paul 5 *ad Sabinum*. Admittedly Grosso thinks that

tackle succession until after obligations and hence not in book 2. See, e.g., Lenel, *Pal.* 1, 251 n. 4. This implies a difference from the order in Gaius' Institutes. On any basis such a divergence is improbable. We should expect succession in book 2. 8. 4. 16 is evidence that it was found there. The main support for my proposal on 8. 4. 16 is the similar proposal for 8. 2. 31. See below, 79 n. 3. The variations between the texts of 8. 4. 16 and J. 2. 3. 4 derive from the compilers adapting the passage more thoroughly in the latter; but there is still no mention of a servitude in the passage. It is implied from the context.

[1] There is a more detailed discussion below, 143.
[2] *Studi Albertoni* 1, 464 ff. at 465 n. 29.

this text is also interpolated, but we need not agree.[1] More importantly, the book 21 *ad edictum* from which 8. 2. 1 pr. comes contains Paul's commentary on the servitude formulae in the edict.[2] It follows that if there was a servitude *altius tollendi*, we should expect Paul to discuss it at this point also.

Solazzi[3] brackets much of the text but all we need to notice at the moment is that he thinks that it originally read *neque itineris actusve neque altius non tollendi servitutem*, the plural *servitutes* having been inserted to refer to both kinds of servitude, *altius non tollendi* and *altius tollendi*. His argument is curious and mistaken but need not detain us, for *servitutes* is correct, since it refers also to *itineris actusve*. *Servitutem* would be wrong.

From the point of view of substance, either the positive or the negative form of the servitude would be an appropriate example, so that there is no reason to doubt the positive form. Besides, as all the other examples are of positive servitudes, the positive *altius tollendi* fits neatly into the text, more neatly than would a negative form. There is no reason on the internal evidence of this text to doubt the reference to the servitude *altius tollendi* and it should be added to the evidence.

The last text which is often cited is 8. 4. 7. 1:

Paul (5 ad Sabinum) interpositis quoque alienis aedibus imponi potest, veluti ut altius tollere vel non tollere liceat [vel etiam si iter debeatur], ut ita convalescat, si mediis aedibus servitus postea imposita fuerit: sicuti per plurium praedia servitus imponi etiam diversis temporibus potest. quamquam dici potest, si tria praedia continua habeam et extremum tibi tradam, vel tuo vel meis praediis servitutem adquiri posse: si vero extremo, quod retineam, quia et medium meum sit, servitutem consistere, sed si rursûs aut id, cui adquisita sit servitus, aut medium alienavero, interpellari eam, donec medio praedio servitus imponatur.

We are concerned with the part down to *temporibus potest*. The words in square brackets are usually thought to be a gloss.[4] *Imponi* in the first clause lacks a subject, but it can be supplied from the end of the principium.[5] Guarneri Citati[6] pointed out that

---

[1] Below, 28.   [2] Lenel, *E.P.* 191. See also below, 91.
[3] *Specie*, 97, repeated and expanded in *Tutela*, 177.
[4] See *Ind. Itp.*   [5] Branca, *Studi Cicu* 1, 116.
[6] 1 (1927) *Annali Messina* 92 ff.

non tollere liceat is an odd construction when taken in conjunction with the preceding *altius tollere* and he wanted to make the text read *ut altius tollere non liceat*, which would eliminate any reference to the positive form of the servitude. That is hardly justified since it is the negative form which is in some degree objectionable here and the most straightforward solution would be to delete *vel non tollere* and leave the positive form. Grosso[1] would rather remove the entire phrase *veluti–liceat* and suppose a major work of reconstruction. These problems combined with the odd reference to *iter* might, however, lead one to suppose not alteration in substance but careless abbreviation and amalgamation.

Solazzi[2] says that the reference to *altius tollendi* is certainly interpolated and besides the formal arguments so far noticed, he makes an objection on substance. It is that while a person who has to abstain from raising his house has an interest to ensure that the *mediae aedes* is subject to the same servitude, the person who permits another to raise his house has no interest to see that the *mediae aedes* is similarly burdened. As Branca remarks,[3] this argument is faulty because Paul is referring to the dominant owner who *altius tollit*.

Two other pieces of evidence point to the existence of a servitude *altius tollendi* and so may be mentioned here though they will not be discussed till later. Firstly, C. 3. 34. 1. If the existence of a servitude *altius tollendi* is denied, a tortured meaning must be given to the words or widespread interpolation has to be assumed. If Caracalla's system included such a servitude the problems are not so great.[4] Secondly, 8. 5. 6. 1, Ulpian 17 *ad edictum*. The words

---

[1] *Studi Albertoni* 1, 462. [2] *Specie*, 97 ff.

[3] *Studi Cicu* 1, 116. Since we have no occasion to return to the text it is as well to note here that the passage can be fitted quite satisfactorily into a system, such as I suppose, where an owner whose house had no servitude *altius non tollendi* in its favour could none the less object to building which affected his light seriously. Suppose three houses A, B, and C in a row. If A arranges to have a servitude *altius tollendi* from C, this will allow him to build if he blocks C's lights and C will have no right to object. On the other hand, if a similar servitude is not imposed on B, the A–C right is of no use since B can stop the building. Hence it would be common sense to make the A–C servitude come into effect only when an A–B servitude was arranged. On such a basis the present text is acceptable.

[4] For discussion see below, 116 ff.

in his servitutibus must be rejected if classical law had only one servitude of light. The text is not happy but the odds are against the compilers substituting this vague phrase which hangs in the air in the Digest. We should expect them to be more explicit. In Ulpian's commentary the words would doubtless be entirely in place. If they are Ulpian's, he not only knew of two servitudes of light but was commenting on the formulae for both in the edict.[1]

Because it is ambiguous we cannot rely on the famous inscription from Pompeii.[2] It dates from about 10 B.C.

> M. Holconius Rufus d(uum) v(ir) i(ure) d(icundo) tert(ium),
> C. Egnatius Postumus d. v. i. d. iter(um),
> ex d(ecreto) d(ecurionum) ius luminum
> opstruendorum HS cIɔ cIɔ cIɔ
> redemerunt, parietemque
> privatum col(oniae) Ven(eriae) Cor(neliae)
> usque at tegulas
> faciundum coerarunt.

Overbeck and Mau[3] are sure that the *ius luminum opstruendorum* is a right to block lights and they argue that this is borne out by the phrase *usque at tegulas* in the next clause. Karlowa agrees.[4] Other scholars reject this interpretation and prefer to take the *ius luminum opstruendorum* as the right to block up windows. The trouble with this is that such a right is not among the recognized servitudes—but this objection may not be conclusive. Although Overbeck and Mau say that *obstruere* with the accusative can mean 'obscure' just as well as *obstruere* with the dative, the only evidence for that is an isolated text of the fifth century A.D.[5] The Pompeii

[1] See below, 92 f. and 110.

[2] C. G. Bruns, *Fontes iuris Romani* (7th edition, edited by Gradenwitz, Tübingen, 1909), no. 141. *C.I.L.* 10 1, no. 787.

[3] J. Overbeck–A. Mau, *Pompeji in seinen Gebäuden, Alterthümern und Kunstwerken dargestellt* (4th edition, Leipzig, 1884), 99; n. 43 on 636 with refs.

[4] *Rechtsgeschichte* 2, 531 n. 1.

[5] Maximus of Turin, *Sermones* 53. 2 (*Corpus Christianorum Series Latina*, edited by A. Mutzenbecher, Turnhout, 1962): *lux enim Christi non parietibus obstruitur non aelementis dividitur non tenebris obscuratur*. The passage is found in J. P. Migne, *Patrologiae Cursus, series Latina* 57 (Paris, 1862), *Homilia* 57. The *Thesaurus* 9 Z, 256 lines 2–5 and 29–31 groups all the passages under the meaning 'to block up', but the editor takes *lumina* in the Pompeii inscription as referring to the spaces between columns. I am grateful to the Director of the *Thesaurus* for making the proofs of the article available to me.

inscription is best left to float, especially since it does not add much even if a servitude *altius tollendi* is in question.

Two other important texts fall to be considered together. I have shown elsewhere[1] that Segrè was wrong in arguing that the terms *actio confessoria* and *actio negatoria* were coined by the compilers; both are classical. It was also pointed out that there is no evidence for the existence of a classical technical term *actio negativa*.[2] Segrè had argued that the compilers substituted *actio negatoria* for a classical *actio negativa*.

The purported discovery of this substitution served to modernize and round off in an apparently neat fashion one of the older theories for dealing with the troublesome *ius altius tollendi*. The particular passages for which this theory was devised are G. 4. 3 and J. 4. 6. 2.

G. 4. 3 in rem actio est cum aut corporalem rem intendimus nostram esse, aut ius aliquod nobis competere, veluti utendi aut utendi fruendi, eundi agendi aquamve ducendi vel altius tollendi prospiciendive: actio ex diverso est negativa.

J. 4. 6. 2 aeque si agat ius sibi esse fundo forte vel aedibus utendi fruendi vel per fundum vicini eundi agendi vel ex fundo vicini aquam ducendi, in rem actio est. eiusdem generis est actio de iure praediorum urbanorum. veluti si agat ius sibi esse altius aedes suas tollendi prospiciendive vel proiciendi aliquid vel immittendi in vicini aedes. contra quoque de usufructu et de servitutibus praediorum rusticorum, item praediorum urbanorum invicem quoque proditae sunt actiones, ut quis intendat ius non esse adversario utendi fruendi, eundi agendi aquamve ducendi, item altius tollendi prospiciendi proiciendi immittendi: istae quoque actiones in rem sunt, sed negativae. quod genus actionis in controversiis rerum corporalium proditum non est: nam in his is agit qui non possidet: ei vero qui possidet non est actio prodita, per quam neget rem actoris esse. sane uno casu qui possidet nihilo minus actoris partes optinet, sicut in latioribus digestorum libris opportunius apparebit.

Modern scholars have had the refuge of interpolation, but this was not open to past generations. When faced with these texts which seem to mention a servitude *altius tollendi*, older writers advanced the theory that these passages show that the actions were not grouped according to their function but according to the

[1] Rodger, 88 (1971) *ZSS* 184.   [2] 88 *ZSS* 211 ff.

structure of their formula. That is to say, the Roman writers did
not gather all the actions claiming a usufruct or servitude in one
group and all those denying one in another. Rather they took all
the actions with formulae *ius esse* . . . together and all the actions
with formulae *ius non esse* . . . together, irrespective of whether the
actions for which the formulae were drafted were claiming or
denying a usufruct or servitude. Any action with the formula
ius esse . . . was known as an *actio confessoria*, any with the formula
ius non esse . . . as an *actio negatoria* (or *negativa*). Support for this
was found in Theophilus and a scholium of Stephanus. It was
frankly admitted that the Digest passages bear witness to a
different classification, where *actio confessoria* refers to a claim for a
servitude, *actio negatoria* to the action denying a servitude.[1]

With the development of interpolation research, the loose ends
of this old theory could be tidied up. Grosso and Boháček give the
fullest accounts of the more sophisticated version.[2] It claims to
explain the existence of different classifications on historical
grounds. The term *actio negativa* is classical; *actio negatoria* and
actio confessoria are Byzantine. G. 4. 3 and J. 4. 6. 2 which classify
the actions according to whether they have an *intentio* with *ius
esse* . . . or an *intentio* with *ius non esse* . . . represent the classical
viewpoint and the term *actio negativa* was used for the second kind
of action. The Byzantines, on the other hand, classified actions
according to their function, i.e. claiming or denying a usufruct,
servitude, etc., and for this new classification they invented the
terminology *actio confessoria* and *actio negatoria*. J. 4. 6. 2 shows
traces of the reform.

This elaborate theory is wrong, but it does indicate roughly the
correct approach to G. 4. 3 and J. 4. 6. 2. What has to be appreciated is that in a servitude action the plaintiff does not claim or
deny the servitude, but rather he claims or denies the right to walk
on someone's land, to lead water over it, to build a house higher,
to put a beam in a neighbour's wall, etc. The decision whether
or not the plaintiff has the right is decided by the judge on the

[1] See, e.g., Schmidt, 15 (1850) *Zeitschrift für geschictliche Rechtswissenschaft*
149, esp. at 159 ff.
[2] Grosso, *Studi Albertoni* I, 477–87. Boháček, 46 (1939) *BIDR* 185–93.

relevant evidence, a major factor in which will be the existence or not of a servitude.[1] This means that the action to deny a servitude *altius non tollendi* is framed as *Ao Ao ius esse altius tollere*—Aulus Agerius' right to build is the result of Numerius Negidius not having a servitude to stop him. Where Grosso and the others go wrong is in saying that the *ius altius tollendi* can refer *only* to the action denying a servitude *altius non tollendi*. If we find a servitude *altius tollendi* in other texts, we are free to say that references to a *ius altius tollendi* can also in appropriate circumstances refer to an action claiming a right to build by virtue of having a servitude which gives this right.

In G. 4. 3 Gaius is explaining that an action is *in rem* when we claim either that a corporeal *res* is ours or that we have a right. He then gives certain examples of these rights: personal servitudes, followed by rustic servitudes and finally *altius tollendi prospiciendive*.[2] In all the cases apart from the last pair, in referring to the real action claiming a right, Gaius is talking about an *actio confessoria*, but when we reach this pair, that need no longer be so since my right to build may depend in the particular circumstances either on the presence of a servitude *altius tollendi* or on the absence of a servitude *altius non tollendi*. Hence the *ius altius tollendi* here does not refer to one of either the servitude *altius tollendi* or the servitude *altius non tollendi* but to both. In just the same way the opponent's action will be negative in either eventuality, because he may deny the right to build in the particular circumstances either on the basis of a servitude *altius non tollendi* or on the basis of the absence of a servitude *altius tollendi* in the builder's favour.

The same is to be said of J. 4. 6. 2, which probably derives from the *res cottidianae*.[3] At the end of J. 4. 6. 1, the writer explains that actions *in rem* are actions about a *res* and he gives the example of Titius claiming a corporeal *res* from a possessor who says he is owner. Titius' action against him to claim the *res* is an action *in rem*. At the start of J. 4. 6. 2 with *aeque si agat* we have a list of actions on rustic servitudes. The *aeque* makes it plain that they are the same kinds of actions as the real action of which the author has

---

[1] See also below, 108.   [2] On prospect, see below, 125 ff.
[3] Ferrini, *Opere* 2, 404 ff.

just spoken; hence they are actions claiming a right as opposed to actions claiming a corporeal *res*. Since all rustic servitudes are positive, no one could deny that when he talks of claiming a *ius* the writer is talking in every case about an *actio confessoria*. With *eiusdem generis est* we are told that the action on urban servitudes is of the same kind and we are given a certain number of examples. If they are of the same kind it means that they too are actions claiming a right, but that in turn means merely that a *ius altius tollendi*, a right to build higher, is being claimed. It does not let us know whether the right is the result of a servitude *altius tollendi* or of the absence of a servitude *altius non tollendi*. It could be either. Precisely the same goes for the next sentence, which talks about actions denying a right to build.

There is no need to posit a historical shift in terminology. *Actio negativa* is not a technical term of classical law and G. 4. 3 and J. 4. 6. 2 are merely talking about types of real actions. The fatal error is to try to argue that because the *ius altius tollendi* could (though in my view wrongly) be explained here merely as a function of the servitude *altius non tollendi*, therefore it is always to be explained thus.[1]

That concludes the examination of the evidence. What is perhaps most striking is the prominence of the *ius altius tollendi*. Modern textbooks refer boldly to the servitude *altius non tollendi* and relegate the servitude *altius tollendi* virtually to footnote status, or even omit it altogether.[2] Present-day writers are embarrassed by it, but ancient writers were not. They give it pride of place.[3] Of the nine texts examined only two, J. 2. 3. 1 and D. 8. 4. 16

[1] It is sufficient for present purposes to state that there is no hint of anything different in Theophilus on J. 4. 6. 2. His most noteworthy innovation is the extension of the *confessoria* terminology to include within it the ordinary *rei vindicatio*; though his commentary is framed from a different standpoint from that of Gaius and Justinian, there is no confusion. The scholium of Stephanus on Basilica 16. 6. 5 does show very slight traces of confusing the two ways of looking at real actions. H. J. Scheltema, D. Holwerda, *Basilicorum Libri LX*, *Series B. vol. III, Scholia in libros XV–XX* (Groningen, 1957), 993. However, there is no reason to project this confusion into the texts of Gaius and Justinian where it is not to be found.

[2] It makes an appearance only in the appendix to the third edition of Jörs–Kunkel, *Römisches Privatrecht*.

[3] This has been noticed before by A. Perret, *Le ius altius tollendi* (thèse, Paris, 1924), 136 and Grosso, *Studi Albertoni* 1, 468.

mention the *ius altius non tollendi* without reference to the *ius altius tollendi*. Both servitudes are found in G. 2. 14, G. 2. 31, G. Ep. 2. 1. 3, D. 8. 2. 2, and 8. 4. 7. 1 (where the reference to the *ius altius non tollendi* is a little doubtful), but in each case *altius tollendi* is mentioned before *altius non tollendi*. Finally in two texts, 8. 2. 1 pr. and 8. 3. 2 pr., the *ius altius tollendi* is given without any reference to *altius non tollendi*.

The prominence of the *ius altius tollendi* means that it is not inferior or secondary to the *ius altius non tollendi*. By the same token, the texts indicate that the *ius altius tollendi* is as much a part of the general legal order as the *ius altius non tollendi* or any other servitude for that matter.

For the moment these reflections are enough. If the servitude *altius tollendi* was in no way secondary to the servitude *altius non tollendi*, we must accept that it existed independently and this confirms the conclusion reached earlier that there is no evidence for a classical doctrine of unrestricted freedom to build.[1] There would be no place for this servitude in a system founded on such a doctrine. The two strands of the argument are interwoven. The task which has to be undertaken in the following chapters is to explain the working of a classical system containing both servitudes, but before that, some attention must be given to the Justinianic position. This section can be brief, since there is less dispute about the facts, even though in their interpretation the emphasis has been wrong.

Justinianic Law

When it emerged from the examination of 8. 2. 9, C. 3. 34. 8, and C. 3. 34. 9 that these texts were unsatisfactory evidence for classical law, simultaneously this told us much about Justinian's law. Hitherto it has always been argued on the strength of these three texts that the classical law knew the doctrine of freedom to build which they enshrine, while the law of Justinian knew one of modification of this freedom partly by statutory restrictions and

---

[1] The only previous hint of an explanation on similar lines is by Grosso, *Studi Albertoni* 1, 468–71, who soon abandons the notion.

partly by the application of 'equitable' decisions.[1] However, if these three texts are interpolated and found in the Corpus Iuris, it follows that they represent the basic Justinianic outlook. This emerges especially clearly in the case of 8. 2. 9 since the text has been deliberately moved from a different context to its present position just to provide a statement of the doctrine of freedom to build.[2] This can be the work of no one except Justinian's compilers.

Though they favoured such freedom, the compilers envisaged it within a framework of statutory restrictions which are available for inspection in the Code. In C. 8. 10. 12. 2 we are told in a constitution of Zeno that a man enjoyed unlimited freedom to build provided he left a gap of twelve feet between his house and the neighbouring one. The main exception to this principle was that unless he were building at a distance of at least one hundred feet he could not cut off a prospect of the sea.[3] If the distance was less than twelve feet an old building could still be replaced, but, as had been laid down by Leo, the old dimensions had to be retained.[4]

Zeno made it clear that these provisions, which were largely for the benefit of private individuals, could be set aside by private pacts or stipulations.[5] These are the arrangements which modern scholars[6] rightly see as explaining the existence of a servitude *altius tollendi* in Justinian's law. It would otherwise be totally inexplicable in the regime depicted in 8. 2. 9. The person with one of these arrangements in his favour will be able to ignore the statutory limitations on his freedom. Though there is a place for such a servitude *altius tollendi* in Justinianic law it was completely different in conception from ordinary servitudes. It is for this reason that, while the servitude *altius tollendi* is referred to in

[1] See, for instance, Kaser, *R.P.R.* 2, 191 ff. with 192 n. 24, and 195.
[2] See above, 8 ff. and further below, 51 ff.
[3] C. 8. 10. 12. 2a with C. 8. 10. 12. 4. See also Harmenopulos, Hexabiblos 2. 4. 51 and below at 129.
[4] C. 8. 10. 12. 1a. I take it that, though slightly ambiguous, C. 8. 10. 12. 3a gives provisions concerning windows when the buildings are ten feet apart.
[5] C. 8. 10. 12. 1b and C. 8. 10. 12. 4b.
[6] For instance, Buckland, *Textbook*, 264 though he is puzzled by the classical position.

general enumerations of servitudes, almost all traces of its existence
have been removed from the edictal commentaries where the
detailed working of any classical version would be discussed.

The Byzantine legislation mitigates the doctrine of freedom to
build which none the less underlies it. Two observations are in
order. Firstly, this mitigation was not merely desirable; it was
necessary. The idea that classical law could have worked with a
principle of unrestricted freedom verges on the absurd. Secondly,
the Byzantine legislation is fairly detailed and precise. It may be
risky then to contend that in addition to this the compilers would
feel at liberty to introduce a large number of arbitrary equitable
decisions. They would be more likely to introduce interpolations
with some bearing on their legislation.

One such is to be found in 8. 2. 14:

> Papirius Iustus (1 de constitutionibus) imperatores Antoninus et
> Verus Augusti rescripserunt in area, quae nulli servitutem debet, posse
> dominum vel alium voluntate eius aedificare intermisso legitimo spatio
> a vicina insula.[1]

There is general agreement that *legitimo spatio* is an interpolation
which is intended to refer to the Byzantine legislation. It is
occasionally suggested that the constitution originally referred to
ambitus, but to suppose the survival of *ambitus* at the end of the
second century is implausible.

The text has been so enormously abbreviated that we have no
way of reconstructing either the facts or the decision,[2] but it is
hoped that the following chapters will give some indication at
least of the kind of system within which the emperors must have
formulated their reply.

What emerges from the survey in this chapter is that the
direction of the development of ancient thinking about the scope of
ownership has been misrepresented in the literature: the classical
has been mistaken for the Justinianic, the Justinianic for the classical. Since it was the compilers who proclaimed the extreme

---

[1] *Ind. Itp.* and *Suppl.* Add for instance Biondi, *Cat.* 50 and 51; Boháček,
46 (1939) *BIDR* 145 n. 6 and 146 n. 8; Solazzi, *Tutela*, 164.
[2] Solazzi is understandably suspicious of *quae nulli servitutem debet*, even
though, as he says, one cannot prove it false.

doctrine of freedom to build, Gierke's rage would have been better directed if he had called such doctrines Byzantine as opposed to Roman. Yet the Byzantine jurists were doing little more than confessing their faith; just like Windscheid they knew that in practice this freedom was circumscribed by all kinds of regulations. The classical lawyers apparently operated with a form of ownership in which the restrictions were inherent. Perhaps even Gierke would have approved of their efforts.

2. THE RIGHT TO LIGHT

THE aim of this chapter is to show that the evidence of the classical texts is consistent with the proposition that it could be unlawful for a man to block his neighbour's lights. An outline of the proposed classical scheme will make the argument easier to follow.

In the classical law, in the absence of a servitude *altius non tollendi* to restrain him, an owner was free to build up his house as high as he wished providing that it did not cut off the light to his neighbour's house to an intolerable extent. He had to leave his neighbour at least enough light for ordinary everyday existence.

An owner who wished to build without having to leave this usual amount of light for his neighbour would have to obtain a servitude *altius tollendi* over his neighbour's land. This would give him the necessary freedom, though certain limits might be set in any given instance. If a neighbour wished to ensure a greater amount of light than the bare minimum he would have to obtain a servitude *altius non tollendi*, after which the servient owner could not raise his house beyond the limits laid down in the servitude. In the case of both servitudes, the exact conditions might vary from case to case.

Where an owner, free from any servitude *altius non tollendi*, built in a way which cut off his neighbour's light to an intolerable degree, he could be prevented from building or could be forced to remove what he had built. There were certain rules about which of the parties would be the plaintiff in such cases. Actions on the servitude were available, as also were the *cautio damni infecti* and *operis novi nuntiatio*.

This classical system is sophisticated and involves nice problems, since the judge will have to decide in any given case whether or not the neighbour's loss exceeds what is reasonable. Possibly just because the system was too subtle it was cast aside at some stage and the Justinianic sources reflect the completely different set-up which was outlined at the end of the last chapter.

Since the dominant view is against any right to light in classical law there is room for two brief preliminary observations which suggest that the Roman jurists were alive to the problem of light in other areas of the law and so cannot be thought *necessarily* to have been indifferent when the matter arose between neighbours.

Firstly, a fructuary could sue the owner of the subjects of the usufruct if the latter blocked his lights and so impaired his enjoyment of the usufruct.[1]

Secondly, under the edict *ne quid in loco publico*,[2] the interdict was available to prevent a structure being raised *in publico* which diminished the plaintiff's supply of light.

43. 8. 2. 11 Ulpian (68 ed edictum) damnum autem pati videtur, qui commodum amittit, quod ex publico consequebatur, qualequale sit. 12. proinde si cui prospectus, si cui aditus sit deterior aut angustior, interdicto opus est. 13. si quid in loco publico aedificavero, ut ea, quae ex meo ad te nullo iure defluebant, desinant fluere, interdicto me non teneri Labeo putat. 14. plane si aedificium hoc effecerit, ut minus luminis insula tua habeat, interdictum hoc competit.

Ulpian is commenting on the clause *qua ex re quid illi damni detur*[3] and more specifically on the notion of *damnum*, loss. In 11, we are told that a person suffers loss if he is inconvenienced in any way. This is a wide definition of *damnum* and from it Ulpian deduces in 12 that the interdict lies if a prospect is made worse or an approach made narrower. On the other hand, in 13 he reports Labeo's opinion that you cannot complain if I build something *in publico* with the result that water, unsecured by a servitude—the servitude in question is not one of the usual ones—no longer flows on to your land.[4] According to 14 it is obvious that you will have a remedy if my building reduces the amount of light which your *insula* receives.

Despite the isolated assault of Riccobono,[5] which was opposed by Bonfante,[6] we have no reason to doubt the authenticity of 14, where Ulpian regards it as almost superfluous to mention that reduction of light will attract a remedy. The cases which interest

---

[1] See the discussion later in this chapter.   [2] Lenel, *E.P.* 458.
[3] 43. 8. 2. 10, Ulpian 68 *ad edictum*. Lenel, *E.P.* 458 n. 10.
[4] On 13 and 14, see below, 49 ff.   [5] 21 (1896) *RISG* 394 n. 1.
[6] Cf. *Ind. Itp.* See also below, 49 ff.

him are those of prospect and *aditus* which are narrower and which
have to be justified by a more extensive interpretation of *damnum*.
Since blocking of lights causes *damnum* here, we must deduce that
it was considered unlawful in this context for we know that 'no one
inflicts loss except someone who does what he has no right to do'.[1]

Clearly then in this context blocking of lights could be unlawful.
In fact Ulpian makes a sweeping assertion which suggests that any
reduction is actionable. *Plane si* frequently masks an excision.
There may therefore have been some qualification in the original,
but if there was not, the easy availability of this remedy may
perhaps be explained by the fact that there was no other way of
protecting light when the troublesome structure was on public
land. If it was on private land, you could take out a servitude to
protect yourself, but not in this situation; so the interdict may give
a remedy in cases of relatively slight obstruction where there
would be none against a neighbour building on private land.

Having noted these two areas where Roman jurists protect a
man's lights without any servitude being involved, we may turn
to see if there is any evidence that they took a similar attitude in
dealing with disputes between neighbours. In other words we are
looking for indications that blocking of lights could be unlawful
in classical law. The discussion of the evidence is divided into
four sections. In the first, texts on *damnum infectum* are examined.
The second and longest part concerns a text of Marcellus, 8. 2. 10,
and this is followed by investigation of 8. 2. 11. There are other
texts which seem to fit more readily into a system which acknow-
ledged an owner's right to light and they form the subject of the
concluding portion of the chapter.

I.   39. 2. 25 must be studied in conjunction with 39. 2. 24. 12
and 26.[2]

39. 2. 24. 12 Ulpian (81 ad edictum) item videamus, quando
damnum dari videatur; stipulatio enim hoc continet, quod vitio aedium
loci operis damnum fit. ut puta in domo mea puteum aperio, quo
aperto venae putei praecisae sunt: an tenear? ait Trebatius non

---

[1] 50. 17. 151, Paul 64 *ad edictum*. Lenel, *Pal.* 1, 1081 and n. 7. See the remarks
of Daube, 76 (1959) *ZSS* 224.
[2] See also above, 9.

teneri me damni infecti: neque enim existimari operis mei vitio damnum tibi dari in ea re, in qua iure meo usus sum. si tamen tam alte fodiam in meo, ut paries tuus stare non possit, damni infecti stipulatio committetur.

h.t. 25 Paul (78 ad edictum) Trebatius ait etiam eum accipere damnum, cuius aedium luminibus officiatur.

h.t. 26 Ulpian (81 ad edictum) Proculus ait, cum quis iure quid in suo faceret, quamvis promisisset damni infecti vicino, non tamen eum teneri ea stipulatione: veluti si iuxta mea aedificia habeas aedificia eaque iure tuo altius tollas, aut si in vicino tuo agro cuniculo vel fossa aquam meam avoces: quamvis enim et hic aquam mihi abducas et illic luminibus officias, tamen ex ea stipulatione actionem mihi non competere, scilicet quia non debeat videri is damnum facere, qui eo veluti [uti— Krüger] lucro, quo adhuc utebatur, prohibetur, multumque interesse utrum damnum quis faciat, an lucro, quod adhuc faciebat, uti prohibeatur. mihi videtur vera esse Proculi sententia.

As Lenel points out, 24. 12 and 26 form part of Ulpian's commentary on the words *quod . . . damnum factum erit* in the praetorian stipulation for *damnum infectum.*[1] Ulpian is discussing when there is *damnum*, loss, within the meaning of that term in the *cautio.* 25 comes from a similar context.

It may be convenient to start by setting the texts in the overall picture of *damnum infectum.*[2] The remedy originated to deal with damage threatened from a neighbouring house which was in danger of collapsing. The plaintiff went to the praetor and if he swore an oath *de calumnia* (39. 2. 13. 3) the praetor would then order the defendant to give a *cautio* promising to reimburse the plaintiff for any loss which he suffered from the defendant's house, land, or work within a certain period of time. If the defendant failed to give the *cautio*, the plaintiff would be allowed by the praetor to enter the defendant's land and later, after a *cognitio*, he would be given possession. It would seem that the praetor might refuse to order the defendant to give a *cautio* in the first place if he thought that the proceedings were without foundation[3] or he could refuse the second *missio* if, *causa cognita*, he decided this was the proper course.

---

[1] *Pal.* 2, 883 n. 3. See also above, 9.
[2] See the account in Karlowa, *Rechtsgeschichte* 2, 1239 ff.
[3] Karlowa, *Rechtsgeschichte* 2, 1250.

The question discussed in 39. 2. 24. 12, *h.t.* 25, and *h.t.* 26 is
what amounts to *damnum* in the field of *damnum infectum*. This
problem might arise, it would seem, in several contexts. Firstly,
for example, a person who was going to be asked to give a *cautio*
could argue that the demand was unfounded since there was no
threat of relevant *damnum*. Secondly, a defendant threatened with
the second *missio* could make the same plea at the praetor's
cognitio. Thirdly, when something had occurred after the *cautio*
had been given and the plaintiff was claiming under it, the defendant could argue that whatever the sufferings of the plaintiff might
be, they did not amount to 'loss' in terms of the *cautio* on which he,
the defendant, should accordingly not be liable.

The three texts in question are presumably cases on the third
of these heads. In other words, the defendant has given a *cautio*—
perhaps for instance at the start of some building operations or
alterations to a house—and the texts are concerned with examin-
ing the kinds of loss which will make him liable on his stipulation.

Two recent interpretations of the texts fall to be considered.
In the first place, Professor Stein nods when dealing with 24. 12.
He is talking about 50. 17. 55 and has occasion to refer to our text:

> For example, D. 39. 2. 24. 12 is concerned with the case where I dig
> a well on my land and in so doing cut into the sources of your well.
> Trebatius holds that I am not liable for *damnum infectum*, since the loss
> was caused to you through no defect of my work in a matter in which I
> was exercising my right, *in ea re in qua iure meo usus sum.*[1]

Stein's paraphrase implies that Trebatius held that I had indeed
caused loss though I would not be liable. But the emphasis is
wrong and Stein has transferred the negative to go with *vitium*.
In fact Ulpian is considering when 'loss' is caused, and he says that
Trebatius thought that in the well case loss was not thought to be
caused by my faulty work, when I was merely exercising my right.[2]
The lawfulness of the action precludes any resultant hardship to
my neighbour being classed as legally significant loss. Trebatius is
therefore saying that when I cut off water from my neighbour's

[1] P. Stein, *Regulae Iuris* (Edinburgh, 1966), 120. See, however, Daube, 76
ZSS 215 and 224.

[2] Trebatius is echoing the words of the stipulation. cf. Lenel, *E.P.* 551 ff.

well he does not suffer *damnum* in the sense in which that word is understood in the sphere of *damnum infectum*.

In 25, Paul reports that Trebatius held that even a person whose lights were blocked suffered *damnum*. Again the obvious explanation is to take this as a mere matter of interpreting the term *damnum* in the stipulation. Trebatius was prepared to include the cutting off of light as falling within the range of *damnum*.

If this is correct, Professor Watson's recent interpretation is incorrect.[1] He treats 25 as basically sound but appears not to wish to take it at face value. According to Watson, 25 does not mean that Trebatius would give an action for *damnum infectum*, when lights were affected. Rather:

> *H.t.* 24. 12 shows him in effect considering when the action will lie and when it will not, although the neighbour had suffered loss. Where the supply of water to a well was cut off, he declares that the neighbour did not suffer *damnum operis mei vitio*. But he would have to concede that the neighbour did suffer *damnum* and that through my activity. Trebatius' original point which became the basis of *h.t.* 25 may well have been that another case of *damnum* to my neighbour through my activity which did not give rise to the action is where his light is affected. This would be a more extreme case, possibly even a *reductio ad absurdum*. Trebatius would then be making the same point which is made by Proculus—also, *inter alia*, in respect of building higher—in *h.t.* 26.

Watson, who fundamentally shares Stein's approach here, introduces as a sort of *tertium quid* in the discussion a case of *damnum* for which no action is given. This is scarcely possible especially at this stage in the commentary on the wording of the praetorian stipulation. *Pace* Watson, 24. 12 does not show Trebatius considering 'when the action will lie and when it will not, although the neighbour has suffered loss'. On the contrary it is a question of *quando damnum dari videatur*. The decision whether or not an action lies is made by seeing whether or not there is *damnum*. There is nothing in the texts to suggest that there could be *damnum* and yet, for some reason or other, no action.

The crucial importance of 25 is also the reason why Watson feels so uncomfortable about it that he takes this rather improbable way out: if Trebatius held that an action lay on the

---

[1] *Property*, 143 ff.

cautio damni infecti for blocking of lights then he must also have thought that blocking lights could be unlawful. This is contrary to the modern view of the classical law and so the text is an awkward one for scholars.

As Daube has put it, 'already the classical jurists occasionally expressed the idea that *damnum* in the sense of actionable causing of loss presupposes unlawfulness';[1] this was one of the occasions. The mere fact that I have given you a promise of compensation will not always make me liable. The loss must be caused wrongfully.

39. 2. 24. 3 Ulpian (81 ad edictum) haec stipulatio utrum id solum damnum contineat, quod iniuria fit, an vero omne damnum, quod extrinsecus contingat? et Labeo quidem scribit de damno dato non posse agi, si quid forte terrae motu aut vi fluminis aliove quo casu fortuito acciderit.

Ulpian asks whether the stipulation deals only with *damnum* which happens *iniuria*—unlawfully, wrongfully[2]—or with all *damnum* which occurs from outside. The form of the answer in this text and the discussion in the succeeding texts down to 24. 11 show that liability was not strict and that the loss must be the result of some kind of wrongdoing.

24. 12, which is linked to this discussion by its opening words, develops the theme. Since the *damnum* must happen *iniuria*, *damnum* cannot result from a lawful act. It is that matter to which the commentary now turns. 24. 12 and 26 must be regarded as a unit. In both texts Ulpian and the jurists whom he cites are concerned with cases where there is no liability on a *cautio* because the act complained of is lawful.

In 24. 12 Ulpian informs us that where I dig a well on my land and so cut off the supply to your well, Trebatius held that I am not liable because I have the right to dig a well and hence this ensuing hardship is not to be taken as *damnum*. If the act is lawful no *damnum* can be inflicted. In 26 Ulpian goes on to give the opinion of Proculus who, he says, held that when someone did something *iure* on his own land, he would not be liable even though

[1] 76 *ZSS* 224.
[2] There is no sign of any trend towards introducing *culpa* here as happened as time went by with the Lex Aquilia. Not that it really makes very much practical difference.

he had given a promise to his neighbour. As examples Proculus has the cases where you build up *iure tuo* next to my buildings and where you lead off my water: even though you do take away my water and block my lights you are not liable on the stipulation, the reason being that a person should not appear to suffer loss when prevented from enjoying an advantage which he has experienced hitherto and there is a great difference between suffering a loss and losing an advantage. Ulpian agrees with Proculus.

It is generally agreed that Pernice was correct when he suggested that the part *scilicet quia-prohibetur* is a gloss or interpolation[1] because it adds nothing which is not found in the part which follows it and it is out of harmony grammatically with the remainder of the sentence. I am not altogether sure, but the point is of little importance for us since the drift of this part of the passage can be seen.

No other part of the text has been suspected in any way and doubtless it is substantially sound. Still, in the first sentence past tenses *faceret* and *promisisset* combine awkwardly with the present *ait*. Probably this is just the result of Ulpian fitting Proculus' opinion into his commentary, but the *quis* and *quid* may point to a degree of generalization.

The problem of 26 is said to be this. Proculus held that the *cautio damni infecti* was not effective in the cases which he discussed. At the outset this opinion—according to Ulpian's account —is founded on the idea that the neighbour is within his rights in cutting off the water and blocking the light—*cum quis iure quid in suo faceret*. . . . The building is done *iure tuo*. However, by the time we reach *multumque interesse* (or *scilicet quia*, if this be genuine), Proculus is basing his decision on a distinction between suffering a loss and losing an advantage. The trouble, it is argued, is that if an act was lawful no hardship ensuing as a result could be considered *damnum* for the purposes of *damnum infectum*. Since that should have been an end of the matter Proculus should not have had to write the later part. Yet this later part is not spurious because it appears correctly in indirect speech. Hence Biondi, for example, gave as his reason for cutting out *scilicet quia-prohibetur* that the

[1] *Labeo* 2 1 (2nd edition, Halle, 1895), 49 n. 2.

argument was superfluous once it was decided that the act was done *iure*.[1] That argument of Biondi does not work since we are left with precisely the same problem in *multumque interesse* to the end. Pernice changed his views radically on 24. 12 and 26 between the two editions of *Labeo* but even in the first edition when he thought that the texts were grappling with the problems of acts done *iure*, Pernice thought that Proculus had (possibly deliberately) avoided formulating his decision in these terms and had preferred instead to frame it in terms of *lucrum* and *damnum*.[2]

It is more likely that we have to do with an attempt by Proculus to spell out his decision that no liability arises under the *cautio* for the results of an act done *iure*. In other words, Proculus is dealing explicitly with situations where the act is lawful and his decision is that there is no liability even though a promise of compensation has been given. He cannot give as his reason for denying liability merely the fact that the act was lawful—that is one of the elements of the problem he is considering—and so he formulates it rather in terms of *damnum* and *lucrum*. The law considers that when a man suffers the cutting off of water or the loss of light due to lawful building, he has been deprived of an advantage (*lucrum*) which he has hitherto been lucky enough to enjoy but he has not suffered any loss (*damnum*).[3] Nor is this argument far removed from the one which says that no lawful act can cause legally significant loss. It is the other side of the coin. The limits of what is lawful are defined by what causes hardship which is intolerable and demands a remedy according to the opinion prevailing in the society at that time. In practical terms this comes to a question of making someone liable. Society does not consider that in these water and light cases the detriment is intolerable and hence to be defined as a *damnum* for which the defendant is liable. Proculus is groping towards a statement in these terms.

Both Trebatius in 24. 12 and Proculus in 26 deal with cases where there is no liability on a *cautio* because the act is lawful.

---

[1] *Diritto romano cristiano* 3 (Milan, 1954), 274.

[2] *Labeo* 2 (1st edition, Halle, 1878), 12; *Labeo* 2 1, 49 n. 2. The discussions are particularly interesting when compared.

[3] The *damnum-lucrum* contrast is found elsewhere, e.g. 47. 2. 72. 1, Javolenus 15 *ex Cassio*. See Daube, *Studi in onore di Siro Solazzi* (Naples, 1948), 116 ff.

Nestling between these cases is one which causes difficulty. After recounting Trebatius' decision on the well Ulpian says that none the less if I dig so deeply on my land that your wall cannot stand I shall be liable. Originally Pernice thought that it was a comment of Ulpian himself to do with abuse of rights but later he came to the conclusion that it is interpolated.[1] Against the syntax Watson attributes the opinion to Trebatius but he declines to investigate the reasoning behind the decision.[2] Pernice's first thoughts were nearer the truth than his second and this comment is Ulpian's. The cases of the well, the wall, and lights are examples of operations which people carry out on their own land and the effects of these operations on the people next door. At an early period it may have been felt that no man could be liable for the results of what he did on his own property: he was acting *in suo* and hence, it would be argued, he could not be acting without right. These texts show that there was a shift in opinion and that by the first century B.C. at the latest jurists were no longer frozen in these old attitudes.[3] Though they still gave no remedy for the well case, as we shall see, they were prepared to grant one for lights.

We may assume that for Ulpian the destruction of the wall is *non iure*. We are not told about the basis of the decision but Ulpian would think that fault may be inferred where someone digs on his own land and so undermines his neighbour's wall: a properly conducted piece of digging will not have this disastrous effect.[4] The seriousness of the consequences is at one and the same time the reason why the digger should be careful not to cause them[5] and the reason why such digging is stigmatized as unlawful. The wall case is no exception to the principle that unlawfulness is a prerequisite of liability for *damnum infectum*.

[1] *Labeo* 2 (1st edition), 13 n. 12; *Labeo* 2 1, 58.   [2] *Property*, 143.
[3] Cf. the decision of Q. Mucius in 9. 2. 31, Paul 10 *ad Sabinum* on which A. Watson, *The Law of Obligations in the Later Roman Republic* (Oxford, 1965), 238 ff. and Daube, *Aspects*, 143, though Kunkel, 49 (1929) *ZSS* 180 ff. remains fundamental.
[4] Cf. the important remarks of Daube, *Aspects*, 157–63.
[5] This is not to suggest that negligence was the standard under *damnum infectum*. Cf. above at 44   n. 2. Watson's remarks on fault on the part of the promisor (*Property*, 142) rest on a mistranslation of Cicero, *Topica* 4. 22. He appears to have overlooked the explanation which was given by Daube, 44 (1950) *Classical Quarterly* 119.

Leaving 26 for the moment, we turn our attention to 25. Watson's approach to it has already been rejected.[1] Trebatius is reported by Paul as saying that even a person whose windows are obscured suffers *damnum*. If it is true that before there is *damnum* for the purposes of *damnum infectum* it must be caused *iniuria*, then it follows that Trebatius must have held that blocking lights could sometimes at least be done *iniuria*, wrongfully. Yet according to the dominant modern doctrine blocking of lights can never be wrongful unless there is a servitude *altius non tollendi* and here there is no mention of any such thing. This text in consequence defeats supporters of the usual view of freedom to build. If the text is thought to be genuine,[2] as indeed it must be, given its position inserted into the Ulpian passage, then an attempt is made to deny that it means what it says.

Solazzi[3] says that the text is abbreviated and that Paul was talking about work in breach of a servitude *altius non tollendi*. The argument against this is simply that there is not the slightest indication of such a qualification in the fragment, nor does the discussion into which it has been inserted suggest that the writer would have had such a qualification in mind. It is also strange that the compilers should have cut out this major qualification. These arguments make Solazzi's interpretation too speculative and indeed most scholars have seen the need to look for something rather better.[4]

In his earlier writings Bonfante[5] followed Burckhard–Glück in arguing that in the original context Trebatius was referring to a *facere in publico* as the source of the harm.[6] This was chosen because

[1] Above, 43.

[2] So, for example, in addition to Watson and Bonfante (see below), Pernice, *Labeo* 2 1, 49 n. 2; Daube, *Studi Solazzi*, 113, who does not advert to these matters. [3] *Specie*, 75 n. 161.

[4] In passing we should notice that Watson's additional argument against the Solazzi type of approach is not cogent. Watson says that if there were a servitude the text 'would offend against the principle evidenced in texts from the Empire that no action lies for *damnum infectum* if another remedy is available'. *Property*, 144 ff. See for instance 39. 2. 13. 10, Ulpian 53 *ad edictum* and the remarks on it below, 111 f. The precise nature of the action there does not matter.

[5] Bonfante, *Scritti* 2 (Turin, 1926), 806 n. 1. I have not seen the passage of Burckhard–Glück. Grosso, *Studi Albertoni* 1, 470 ff. saw the correct solution but his nerve failed and he took refuge in the Burckhard–Glück view.

[6] See Lenel, *E.P.* 372 and n. 13.

it is known that people whose light was affected by structures *in loco publico* could recover under the interdict *ne quid in loco publico*.[1] But there is nothing in the text which supports such an idea or hints at such a qualification; nor is it obvious that the same term *damnum* could be interpreted to cover loss of light due to one sort of structure but not that due to another. Bonfante was aware of the weaknesses of this theory and so later he more or less abandoned it to take up the less tenable view, similar to the one previously canvassed by Riccobono, that the text is interpolated.[2] Neither theory will do. The text is genuine. Trebatius held that in certain circumstances at least it was unlawful to block your neighbour's lights and that he suffered *damnum* if you did.

Against this conclusion, which is also reached by Pernice, Bonfante argued on the strength of 24. 12 that Trebatius, who held that cutting off water caused no *damnum*, could not consistently have held that cutting off light did. Any distinction would be illogical, he says, because the cases are parallel: in each an owner by work on his own land prevents some element from reaching his neighbour's land.

Bonfante's argument is not borne out by the texts and for Ulpian at least just such a distinction was possible in the area of the edict *ne quid in loco publico*: 43. 8. 2. 13 and 14.[3] In 13 we are told that Labeo considered that if I build something *in publico* which prevents water flowing from my land to your land I am not liable under the interdict. Ulpian does not express disagreement. In 14, however, he says that 'obviously' I shall be liable if a structure which I build cuts down the light to your block of flats. Ulpian saw a distinction. Bonfante says that the reason why no action is given in the water case is that the water comes from the defendant's land and merely crosses the public land. This is not convincing because the edict is concerned with loss arising out of something done *in loco publico*, and here any loss would arise from the structure put up in the public place. It is this which cuts off the water and so causes the harm. These texts on the interdict suggest that

[1] Cf. 43. 8. 2. 14, Ulpian 68 *ad edictum.*
[2] Bonfante, *Corso* 2 1, 344. Riccobono, 21 (1896) *RISG* 394 n. 1.
[3] Set out above at 39.

the jurists saw a distinction between cutting off a source of water and cutting off light. There can be no reason to reject 25 on this basis: rather the reverse, since it preserves a subtle distinction.

Technical reasons may have been an important factor for the older jurists when they made such distinctions. They may have felt that *officere* (*ob-facere*) was a slightly more active invasion of the neighbour's sphere than merely diverting, *avocare* and *praecidere*, so that interference with a neighbour was more positive in the former case and merited a remedy. Just in the same way there is liability if a man digging on his own land causes his neighbour's wall to fall down—somehow there is also in this instance a more positive intrusion.

A trace of such attitudes may have lingered on and influenced the thinking even of later classical jurists, but probably a more important reason at least for retaining the distinction would be that it reflects the conditions of Roman life in which to be deprived of light was more serious than to be deprived of water. Losing daylight could be an essentially irremediable disaster since in the absence of any efficient artificial light there was no alternative source of supply. Losing a source of water would not be quite so bad. We can deduce from what the *agrimensores* say[1] in connection with the *actio aquae pluviae arcendae* that the problem in Italy was not that there was too little water but rather that there was too much. This suggests that there would usually be a fair amount of rain providing an adequate supply of water, so that while it would often be a considerable advantage to receive water from a neighbour's land, only rarely would it be disastrous not to have such water. While any alternative arrangement—perhaps storing water or leading it in from some other stream in the area—might prove costly and tiresome, the situation would be in essence remediable whereas the light case would not. Such considerations could have led the jurists to distinguish the cases and to hold that a man was within his rights in cutting off water which reached his neighbour from his land but not in cutting off light.

[1] Frontinus in F. Blume–K. Lachmann–A. Rudorff, *Die Schriften der römischen Feldmesser* i (Berlin, 1848), 36 and 57.

In the discussion so far, we have argued that in *damnum infectum* the act giving rise to the detriment must be wrongful or else there is no liability or, to put it another way, no *damnum* (39. 2. 24. 3). 39. 2. 24. 12 and 26 are about cases where the act is lawful (*iure*) and various jurists say there is no liability. In 25, Paul reports Trebatius to the effect that loss of light amounts to *damnum*. Hence for Trebatius at least blocking of lights could be unlawful.

8. 2. 9 introduces a further complication.[1] Some remarks have already[2] been made on the palingenesia of the passage. The text probably comes from a discussion of the scope of the word *damni* in the edict *de damno infecto* but the precise context is hard to pinpoint. It will probably not be quite the same as for 39. 2. 24. 12, *h.t.* 25 and *h.t.* 26 because they are texts on the praetorian stipulation itself. The matter could arise in practice when the praetor was considering whether to order the defendant to give a *cautio*; it might perhaps recur when the praetor was deciding in the *cognitio* whether to order a second *missio in possessionem*. A further possibility arises from the fact that if the defendant ignores the demand for the *cautio* and then does not allow the plaintiff to enter into possession, he is liable on a fictitious action[3] for the amount he would have had to pay if he had given the *cautio*. At this point the defendant could argue that he would not have been liable at all since the harm done would not be termed *damnum* within the scope of the *cautio*. Our text could relate to any of these situations.

As the text now stands, it says that there is no action against a person who by building darkens his neighbour's house to which he does not owe a servitude. Whatever the course adopted in interpreting this text, it will not affect the fundamental point[4] that the text cannot be taken as showing that a man has an unlimited right to build. The discussion can only be about the scope of Ulpian's remarks in relation to *damnum infectum*.

In its present state, 8. 2. 9 appears to mean that Ulpian was not prepared to allow an action on *damnum infectum* for blocking lights. If that was indeed what Ulpian said, he took a different

---

[1] The text is set out above, 8.   [2] At 8 ff.
[3] Lenel, *E.P.* 373.   [4] See above, 9 ff.

line from Trebatius—and possibly even Paul—in 39. 2. 25. There
is no harm in that: Trebatius could take one position and Ulpian
another. But the opinion of Ulpian in 8. 2. 9 must also be set
beside that of Proculus in 39. 2. 26 with which he expresses his
agreement.

Trebatius thought that blocking lights could sometimes be
unlawful. In 26, Proculus gives as an act done *iure*, 'if you had a
building next to mine and you raised it *iure tuo*', and he says there
is no liability on the stipulation for any resulting diminution in the
neighbour's light. Supporters of the customary doctrine of freedom
to build have little trouble with this example: for them blocking of
lights is always lawful in default of a servitude. Hence they could
say that in 8. 2. 9 Ulpian is denying liability on the *cautio* because
blocking of lights is lawful and *damnum* for *damnum infectum*
presupposes unlawfulness. The crucial evidence against that
approach is 25. The question is then whether or not it is acceptable
to say that Trebatius could hold the blocking of lights to be
wrongful while the later Proculus with Ulpian would hold it
lawful. My feeling is that the lawfulness or otherwise of cutting off
another person's light would be too important a topic for there to
be much dispute among the jurists. They would have decided one
way or the other and it seems unlikely that classical jurists would
have reversed an earlier decision that it was unlawful. Does 26
definitely mean that Proculus and Ulpian decided that blocking
was always lawful?

The answer is that it does not prove so much. As was seen
previously[1] 24. 12 and 26 deal expressly with the problem of
whether there can be *damnum* where the act is done *iure*. The
problems which Proculus poses are framed to put this question
and so he must set up precisely those situations where the act is
lawful. When he sets out the light case he is careful to state that the
building is done *iure tuo*—the builder was 'within his rights'.[2]
On the usual approach which assumes that blocking is always
lawful, these words are superfluous. Grosso thinks that they are an
unnecessary gloss or interpolation.[3] If so, why should anyone

---

[1] At 44 f.   [2] Daube, *Studi Solazzi*, 113.
[3] *Studi Albertoni* 1, 471 n. 39.

bother to insert them? The words must mean something and though they are rather ambiguous they suggest that blocking could be unlawful. They cannot, I think, be taken as meaning that the building is lawful because there is no servitude *altius non tollendi* to prevent it. If that were the meaning, then the words could have occurred equally well in the water case.[1] Yet they do not appear in either of the accounts of that case.

Two explanations are possible. They could simply mean that the builder was within his rights, and hence even if he was blocking his neighbour's lights he was not doing so excessively. In other words, a defendant would be liable only if he built in excess of his rights. That would be the situation envisaged in 25. Where he built within his rights there would be no liability. That would be what Proculus and Ulpian are saying in 26. Alternatively, we may suggest that the words *iure tuo* refer to a servitude—the builder has a servitude right to build higher, a servitude *altius tollendi*. Since he has a servitude, his building is lawful and so even if the result is that his neighbour's lights are blocked, the latter has no redress. There is no need to see any clash between 25 and 26.

If that explanation of 26 is accepted, it does pose certain problems for 8. 2. 9 since neither Proculus nor Ulpian would rule out liability on the *cautio* for loss due to deprivation of light. Yet in its present form 8. 2. 9 would seem to rule it out absolutely. 8. 2. 9 has been the victim of even more generalization than we have hitherto supposed. The main change of meaning was effected by placing the text in its new context, but we also said, following Solazzi in this, that the clause *quibus non serviat* was probably an addition of the compilers to fit the text into its new surroundings in a title on servitudes. In order to square it with the interpretation of 26 which has been advanced, we should suggest that Ulpian originally wrote something like:

cum eo qui iure suo usus tollendo obscurat vicini aedes nulla competit actio.

The compilers would have cut out *iure suo usus* and inserted the extra clause, which they might indeed have seen—though wrongly

---

[1] Cf. 43. 18. 2. 13, Ulpian 68 *ad edictum*.

—as restating the sense of the words which they were removing. Such a change is conceivable and not very drastic. It is easier also to assume that some such alteration was made not only because the text is in the *sedes materiae* but also because the repositioning shows that the compilers were particularly interested in this text and in generalizing its meaning.

There are certain other matters to be taken into account when trying to understand the position. The second of the praetorian stipulations for *damnum infectum* listed by Lenel, *quod aedium loci operisve vitio damnum factum erit* ran:[1]

quod aedium loci operisve q.d.a. vitio, si quid ibi ruet scindetur fodietur aedificabitur, in aedibus meis intra . . . damnum factum erit, quanti ea res erit, tantam pecuniam dari dolumque malum abesse afuturumque esse spondesne? spondeo.

Lenel thinks that the series of words *ruet, scindetur*, etc., is reminiscent in its style and enumeration of the similar groupings in the Lex Aquilia and that this indicates that the stipulation is ancient. This may well be correct despite Watson's observation that such lists are not necessarily indicative of great age and that this form may not be sufficient to justify assuming that the *cautio* is very old.[2] According to him, the earliest evidence for the *cautio* dates from 73–70 B.C.[3] From G. 4. 31 it seems that the stipulations are to be associated with the praetorian as opposed to the *legis actio* procedure and also that under the former the scope of the action was wider.

Daube has pointed out that it was the width of the term *damnum* which allowed the extension of the remedy beyond the scope of the original rules under which physical damage only had been contemplated.[4] I think that the *cautio* as preserved for us envisages blocking of lights. My reason for suggesting it is that the *cautio* contains the word *aedificabitur*. Unfortunately the compilers cut away the commentaries on these words[5] and so their scope is uncertain. Yet it is difficult to see what the specific word *aedificabitur* could have covered except some sort of blocking either of

[1] Lenel, *E.P.* 551 ff.
[2] *Property*, 126 ff. On such lists see Daube, 20 (1970) *Buffalo Law Review*, 41 ff.   [3] *Property*, 141.
[4] *Studi Solazzi*, 113.   [5] See Lenel, *E.P.* 552 n. 1.

water or of light (also causing an increase in a flow of water), for how else could building by a neighbour cause someone loss in a way not already dealt with by the other words? The examples preserved in the Digest for the interdict *ne quid in loco publico* show that these were the cases which occurred in that context.[1] If the *etiam* in 39. 2. 25 means that Trebatius' opinion was extreme, then it could be that blocking of light was not covered by the *cautio* before the last century of the Republic. The position of *aedificabitur* at the end of the list indicates that it may be a late-comer and this would be in keeping with what we see in 25. If *aedificabitur* does have this scope it would scarcely have become a regular part of the praetorian stipulation while a whole group of jurists, including Ulpian, still refused to give it any effect. Nor is there any obvious reason why they should have set out deliberately to narrow the scope of the *cautio*.

It might be argued that *aedificabitur* was added to operate where there was a servitude *altius non tollendi*, but not otherwise. Yet there is no indication of that qualification and, more importantly, the argument must be based on a feeling that without a servitude an owner does not suffer financially if his light is cut off. Such a notion is questionable.

In the same way, if Ulpian[2] finds it self-evident that blocking lights is covered by the *damnum* in the interdict *ne quid in loco publico*, is it not at least likely that he would favour including it in the *damnum* of *damnum infectum*? This argument cannot be pressed too far since it depends on how strictly *damnum* is interpreted in each case. Not only could such interpretations differ but we are told specifically that the interpretation for the interdict was loose, embracing loss of *commodum*,[3] although this is stated in relation to prospect, the case of lights being regarded as *a fortiori* and almost too banal to be worth mentioning.[4]

The wording of the *cautio* and Ulpian's attitude on the interdict are sufficient to make me prefer an explanation which says that

---

[1] Cf. 43. 8. 2. 6 and 11–15, Ulpian 68 *ad edictum.*

[2] 43. 8. 2. 14, Ulpian 68 *ad edictum.*

[3] 43. 8. 2. 11, Ulpian 68 *ad edictum.*

[4] Julian includes light in the *cautio damni infecti* in 39. 2. 13. 10, Ulpian 53 *ad edictum* and there is no sign that Ulpian dissents. On the text see below, 111 f.

Ulpian—and doubtless Proculus also—would have included excessive blocking of lights among the sources of liability for *damnum infectum*. Trebatius certainly did so. He must therefore have considered that such blocking was unlawful. The matter of liability for *damnum infectum* is not in itself vital for our purposes except that it indicates that the jurists could see blocking as unlawful. Since Trebatius' opinion definitely goes in this direction and cannot be shaken, while no other except 8. 2. 9 is irretrievably against it, we should accept that in classical law excessive blocking of lights was regarded as wrongful.

II. Although 8. 2. 10 is always cited as showing that the unlawfulness of blocking lights is a Byzantine innovation,[1] when properly understood it indicates that the classical jurists knew about the need to leave a neighbour a reasonable amount of light. This means that failure to do so, that is excessive blocking, was unlawful.

8. 2. 10 Marcellus (4 digestorum) Gaurus Marcello: binas aedes habeo, alteras tibi lego, heres aedes alteras altius tollit et luminibus tuis officit: quid cum illo agere potes? et an interesse putes, suas aedes altius tollat an hereditarias? et de illo quaero, an per alienas aedes accessum heres ad eam rem quae legatur praestare debet, sicut solet quaeri, cum usus fructus loci legatus est, ad quem locum accedi nisi per alienum non potest. Marcellus respondit: qui binas aedes habebat, si alteras legavit, non dubium est, quin heres alias possit altius tollendo obscurare lumina legatarum aedium: idem dicendum est, si alteri aedes, alteri aliarum usum fructum legaverit. non autem semper simile est itineris argumentum, quia sine accessu nullum est fructus legatum, habitare autem potest et aedibus obscuratis. ceterum usu fructu loci legato etiam accessus dandus est, quia et haustu relicto iter quoque ad hauriendum praestaretur. sed ita officere luminibus et obscurare legatas aedes conceditur, ut non penitus lumen recludatur, sed tantum relinquatur, quantum sufficit habitantibus in usus diurni moderatione.

This text cannot be studied in isolation from 7. 1. 30:

Paul (3 ad Sabinum) si is, qui binas aedes habeat, aliarum usum fructum legaverit, posse heredem Marcellus scribit alteras altius tollendo obscurare luminibus, quoniam habitari potest etiam obscuratis

[1] For example, P. Bonfante, *Istituzioni* (10th edition, reprinted Turin, 1946), 320 n. 2; Kaser, *R.P.R.* 2, 192 n. 24.

aedibus. quod usque adeo temperandum est, ut non in totum aedes obscurentur, sed modicum lumen, quod habitantibus sufficit, habeant.

Over the years much[1] has been written about 8. 2. 10. Since the time of Pernice,[2] there has been complete agreement that the last part of 8. 2. 10 *sed ita . . . moderatione* is a Justinianic interpolation, while equally all scholars, with the exception of Kreller,[3] have agreed that the same must be said for *quod usque adeo . . . habeant* in 7. 1. 30. Despite this consensus of opinion, close inspection of the texts suggests that the accepted view is too simple. It stands partly on grounds of substance, partly on grounds of form. We start with considerations of form.

At the outset, it must be noted that if these sections are interpolated, then they must be, as is generally assumed, the work of Justinian's compilers. 8. 2. 10 is from Marcellus 4 *digestorum*, while 7. 1. 30 is from Paul 3 *ad Sabinum*. The language of the disputed parts is so similar that it is hard to believe that they could be written completely independently of each other. To believe in a non-Justinianic interpolation of the text, we should have to suppose one of three things. Firstly, the two books were interpolated by the same pre-Justinianic writer and the compilers just happened to use his editions of these two works for excerpting both texts. Secondly, the texts were interpolated by two different hands but one was relying on the work of the other and again the compilers chanced to use these versions. Although neither sequence of events is inconceivable, neither is likely. The only other vague possibility is that there was some legislation on the topic and various revisers followed it. However, no relevant pre-Byzantine legislation is known and it is dangerous to invent any, while Byzantine scholars would have been unlikely to interfere with the texts transmitted to them. Thus the two main possibilities are that the sections are classical or that they are Justinianic, with a remote chance that they could reflect the language of legislation.

---

[1] See *Ind. Itp.* and *Suppl.* Add, e.g., Beseler, 56 (1936) *ZSS* 85 ff.; Kreller, *Deutsche Landesreferate zum II. Int. Kongress für Rechtsvergleichung im Haag 1937* (Berlin and Leipzig, 1937), 11 ff.; Grosso, *Studi Albertoni* 1, 457 n. 4; *Usufrutto*, 200 n. 2; Kaser, *R.P.R.* 2, 192 n. 24.

[2] *Labeo* 2 1, 58; 65 n. 4.

[3] *Deutsche Landesreferate*, 12 n. 5.

35. 2. 2 purports to come from Marcellus 22 *digestorum* and its language is strikingly like that of the disputed part of 8. 2. 10 which is from book 4 of the same work.

Marcellus (22 digestorum) nec amplius concedendum erit, quam quod sufficiat ad speciem modicam monumenti.

8. 2. 10 has *conceditur . . . sufficit . . . moderatione* (this being rendered in 7. 1. 30 as *modicum*); 35. 2. 2 has *concedendum . . . sufficiat . . . modicam*. Such close resemblance suggests that the authors were one and the same. Putting the matter at its lowest, from the standpoint of style any writer who wrote 35. 2. 2 could also have written 8. 2. 10.

35. 2. 2 allows us to banish the hypothesis of legislation. The subject-matter of 35. 2. 2 is the Lex Falcidia and similarity of language between 8. 2. 10 and 35. 2. 2 cannot be explained by supposing different revisers following the same piece of legislation. There is accordingly no reason to suppose that that is the explanation of the similarity between 8. 2. 10 and 7. 1. 30.

We can be more or less sure that 35. 2. 2 was written by Marcellus himself or by a post-classical writer. The text is short and has been moved from the Edictal Mass to its present position between two texts of the Papinianic Mass. It would make no sense to argue that the compilers wrote this sentence, assigned it to Marcellus, and then moved it from one mass to another. We have instead what must be at least a kernel of genuine Marcellus, although there was probably more to it in the original than now meets the eye.[1]

Both 8. 2. 10 and 35. 2. 2 purport to be by Marcellus and to come from the same work. Their language has common elements which make it likely that they are by the same hand. 8. 2. 10 can be either classical or Justinianic, 35. 2. 2 classical or post-classical but not Justinianic. The conclusion is that these linguistic grounds speak for a classical origin of both texts.

The usual formal arguments[2] lose nearly all their force in the light of that conclusion. They are not particularly strong anyway. Suspicions of the word *modicum* tend to be exaggerated, and though

---

[1] See Rodger, 89 (1972) *ZSS*.
[2] See, above all, Riccobono, 21 (1896) *RISG* 397 n. 1.

often spurious, it should not be regarded as an invariable sign of interpolation.[1] If it is genuine in 7. 1. 30, Marcellus could use such expressions. That will further confirm the genuineness of the substance at least of *in usus diurni moderatione* in 8. 2. 10 for which we have just argued. Riccobono objects to *lumen* in 7. 1. 30 being used for 'light' after the plural being used earlier for 'windows'. This is not serious. He also objects to *habitantibus* where the text spoke of the legatee. This is more interesting.[2] In 8. 2. 10 he notes the repetition of *officere* and *obscurare* and the use of *penitus*, a popular word with the compilers. These are plausible arguments but not strong enough to defeat the reasoning in favour of a classical origin.

The upshot is that the texts must be examined in a way which takes these sections into account. 8. 2. 10 is difficult to understand because it has been drastically abridged by the compilers. It is partly at least this abridgement which makes the disputed section look so out of place and so like an appendix which has been added to genuine Marcellus.

The Owner and the Fructuary's Right to Light

7. 1. 30 is usually treated superficially and more or less as an afterthought to the main problem of 8. 2. 10. It is salutary to begin by looking at 7. 1. 30 on its own. Bonfante, Riccobono, Biondi, and Solazzi, for example, cite it specifically in conjunction with 8. 2. 10 as evidence about the right of a person to build and block his neighbour's lights.[3] The text has nothing to do with this. It comes from Paul's third book *ad Sabinum* where he was discussing legacies of usufruct,[4] and more particularly the rights and duties of an heir *vis-à-vis* a fructuary under the legacy. Lenel well compares 7. 6. 1. 1–4, a passage of Ulpian 18 *ad Sabinum*.[5] What Paul is dealing with in 7. 1. 30 is the question whether an heir can build in such a way that he blocks the fructuary's lights, and this is

[1] I hope to be able at some time to publish the results of a survey of some at least of the relevant texts.

[2] See below, 75.

[3] Bonfante, *Istituzioni*, 320 n. 2; Riccobono, 21 *RISG* 395; Biondi, *Cat.* 228; Solazzi, *Specie*, 72 ff.

[4] Lenel, *Pal.* 1, 1258.

[5] *Pal.* 1, 1258 n. 7. See also 1257 n. 2. See further below, 70 ff.

altogether different from the problem of someone blocking a
neighbour's lights. Paul quotes the opinion of Marcellus that the
heir can block the lights since it is possible to live even where a
house is darkened. But, he adds, the house is not to be darkened
completely: a sufficiency of light should be allowed to the people
living in it.

Paul's concern in 7. 1. 30 is the scope of the legatee fructuary's
actions against the heir. This emerges from Lenel's comparison with
7. 6. 1. 1–4 which also dealt with the scope of the actions;[1] but the
compilers eradicated[2] the different types of legacy and with them
discussion of the actions. The matter could also be raised by the
fructuary's real action and the same problem recurs in a text of
Ulpian, reporting a decision of Marcellus' slightly older contem-
porary, Julian:

43. 25. 1. 4 Ulpian (71 ad edictum) item Iuliano placet fructuario
vindicandarum servitutium ius esse: secundum quod opus novum
nuntiare poterit vicino et remissio utilis erit. ipsi autem domino
praedii si nuntiaverit, remissio inutilis erit: neque sicut adversus
vicinum, ita adversus dominum agere potest ius ei non esse invito se
altius aedificare. sed si hoc facto usus fructus deterior fiat petere usum
fructum debebit. idem Iulianus dicit de ceteris, quibus aliqua servitus
a vicino debetur.

39. 1. 2 Julian (49 digestorum) si autem domino praedii nuntiaverit,
inutilis erit nuntiatio: neque enim sicut adversus vicinum ita adversus
dominum agere potest ius ei non esse invito se altius aedificare: sed
si hoc facto usus fructus deterior fiet, petere usum fructum debebit.

The double transmission makes it likely that the relevant part of
these texts is genuine, whatever may be thought of the remainder of
43. 25. 1. 4. This genuine part is overlooked in the standard works
on the subject which are interested merely in Julian's view on the
availability of the *vindicatio servitutis* to the fructuary.[3] Julian held
that if the owner raised a building and as a result the usufruct
deteriorated, the fructuary could sue for this on his real action.
The fructuary must, in other words, be given enjoyment of his

---

[1] See O. Lenel, *Das Sabinussystem* (Strasbourg, 1892), 42 ff.
[2] C. 6. 43. 1. Buckland, *Textbook*, 337.
[3] e.g. Grosso, *Usufrutto*, chapter 6.

usufruct and if cutting off his light reduces his enjoyment he can sue.

At first sight, it might look as if Julian's test here was altogether different from the one in 7. 1. 30: for Julian it is sufficient to found an action if blocking lights makes the usufruct *deterior*, while Paul citing Marcellus insists only that the fructuary be left enough light to live by. Indeed, it is quite probable that Julian's opinion is more favourable to the fructuary. But caution is in order. *Deteriorem facere* is an expression used frequently in the context of usufruct and elsewhere; it measures the limit of the powers of owner and fructuary towards one another. The fructuary must act as a *bonus vir* and this is interpreted as not making the subject of the usufruct *deterior*;[1] the owner also must not make the condition of the usufruct *deterior*.[2] Among other examples of what can amount to rendering *deterior* by the owner are knocking down a building,[3] cutting trees,[4] and imposing servitudes or releasing a neighbour from servitudes.[5] These are unfortunately not sufficient to allow any firm judgement to be made on just how substantial the injury to the fructuary's interests had to be before it could be said that his usufruct had been made *deterior*, but all suggest an appreciable interference with enjoyment. Presumably Julian has that in mind also when talking about blocking lights in 43. 25. 1. 4. At all events, he was in favour of protecting the fructuary's light; the only question can be whether he was more liberal (from the fructuary's point of view) than Marcellus.

Linguistic arguments favoured the attribution of the last part of 7. 1. 30 to Marcellus as reported by Paul. To those arguments may now be added this important one of substance. Cutting out the last part would result in a harsh clash between Julian and the later Marcellus, with Marcellus adopting a curiously rigid position in permitting an owner to ruin a usufruct by cutting off its light entirely—this even though Pomponius had said that merely to cut

---

[1] e.g. 7. 9. 1. 3, Ulpian 79 *ad edictum*.
[2] e.g. 7. 1. 17. 1, Ulpian 18 *ad Sabinum*.
[3] 43. 24. 15. 8, Ulpian 71 *ad edictum* and 7. 6. 2, Pomponius 5 *ad Sabinum*.
[4] 7. 6. 2. Cf. 43. 24. 13 pr., Ulpian 71 *ad edictum*.
[5] 7. 6. 2. See also 7. 1. 16, Paul 3 *ad Sabinum*; *h.t.* 17. 1; *h.t.* 65, Pomponius 5 *ex Plautio* and cf. 11. 3. 9. 1, Ulpian 23 *ad edictum*. In general on the owner's powers, see Grosso, *Usufrutto*, chapter 6.

down trees could be enough to make the owner liable.[1] It is unfair
to burden Marcellus with such nonsense and we can rather assume
that he did say that the owner must leave a sufficiency of light to
the fructuary.

The examination of the fructuary's rights in 7. 1. 30 paves the
way for an investigation of 8. 2. 10. It comes from book 4 of
Marcellus' *digesta* where he was seemingly concerned with
servitudes.[2] The text preserves an account of certain questions
which were put to Marcellus by another jurist, Gaurus.[3] Since the
questioner was a jurist, the questions cannot have been naïve and
must have raised sensible queries. Firstly, I have two houses and I
leave you one by legacy. The heir raises the one in the *hereditas* and
so blocks your lights. What remedy have you against him?
Secondly, does it make any difference whether the heir raises the
house in the estate or another one which he owns? Thirdly, should
the heir offer access to the legatee's house through a third party's
house? A similar point, we are told, arises when a usufruct has been
left of a place which cannot be reached except through the land of
a third party. Marcellus replied that there is no doubt that the heir
can block the legatee's lights by raising the house in the estate.

In the text so far, Gaurus by his first question is in effect
asking whether or not there is a servitude *altius non tollendi*
implied in favour of the legatee over the house of the heir. This is
clear from the origin of the passage in Marcellus' discussion of
servitudes. Furthermore, even though 8. 2. 10 does not specifically
mention servitudes, other texts on similar matters do.

The article by Riccobono 'La destinazione del padre di famiglia'
of which his discussion of 8. 2. 10 forms a part has had great
influence in persuading scholars that all tacit constitutions of
servitudes are Justinianic, but Grosso[4] and more recently Astolfi[5]
have rightly urged that Riccobono's approach was too radical.
Only two examples need be mentioned. In 8. 5. 20 pr., Scaevola 4
digestorum we are given the problem of a testatrix who bequeathed

---

[1] 7. 6. 2.   [2] Lenel, *Pal.* 1, 594.
[3] On him see W. Kunkel, *Herkunft und soziale Stellung der römischen Juristen*
(2nd edition, Graz, Vienna, Cologne, 1967), 214 ff.
[4] 42 (1934) *BIDR* 326.   [5] 23 (1957) *SDHI* 345.

a farm but not two farm houses (*casae*) attached to the farm. In the present state of the text, the question was whether, if the legatee vindicated the farm, the farm should be subject to a servitude to the houses, or if the legatee claimed on the strength of a *fidei-commissum*, the heirs should except a servitude for the houses. The reply is given: *respondit deberi*. Even allowing for the text being from Scaevola with all that means in the way of poor formulation and brevity, we can hardly accept the text as it stands.[1] Riccobono changed *deberi* to *non debere*. That is scarcely to be allowed, but Justinian's reforms of testamentary succession have had an effect. Here are the remains of two distinct questions, the first posed in terms of a legacy *per vindicationem*, the second for *fideicommissum*. In the first case, since the legatee owns the *fundus* the question is put in terms of whether that *fundus* owes a servitude; in the second case, prior to transferring it, the heirs own the *fundus* and the houses so that the question is whether the heirs ought to withhold a servitude. The reply in the text will just about fit the form of the first question, but will not do for the second, and one has to reckon with the likelihood that originally the questions were separate and that Scaevola's reply was given first to the one and then to the other. The compilers have simplified matters and provided both questions with a single answer. There is on the other hand no reason to doubt that Scaevola favoured a servitude in each case.[2] The situation in 8. 5. 20 pr. is the reverse of the primary one in 8. 2. 10 concerning, as it does, the rights of the heir against a legatee rather than the other way about. In 33. 3. 1, Julian 1 *ex Minicio*, two shops, which had previously belonged to the same person, were bequeathed to two different people, and the upper one had something resting on the lower. Was there a servitude *oneris ferendi* between the shops? Minicius thought so, but Julian was rather more doubtful unless it was set up expressly or the legacy was in the form '*tabernam meam uti nunc est do lego*'.[3] For reasons which will emerge in connection with 30. 44. 9 Julian must be contemplating a situation where the thing which rests on

---

[1] For lit., see Astolfi, 23 *SDHI* 352 n. 14 and now Grosso, *Servitù*, 223 ff.

[2] Rather surprisingly Grosso, *Servitù*, 224 uses the brevity of the reply as an indication that it is spurious. The passage is, however, from Scaevola.

[3] Hardly interpolated. Kaser, *R.P.R.* 2, 218 n. 31. Grosso, *Servitù*, 221 ff.

the lower shop is not essential to the existence of the upper shop; the servitude would be a convenience rather than a necessity. Otherwise, given an unco-operative lower owner, Julian's ruling could have virtually the effect of nullifying the legacy of the upper shop.

One may observe that the text of 8. 2. 10 makes out that Gaurus asked what action could be brought—*quid cum illo agere potes?* Older editors who wanted to change this to *num quid* are followed, if not altogether confidently, by Mommsen and Lenel.[1] That suggestion springs from a deep-rooted feeling that there could not possibly be an action. However, matters are not so simple as to justify that emendation, and anyway such a question itself from a jurist would indicate a doubt on the matter.

Marcellus' reply to the first question is that there is no doubt the heir can block the legatee's lights and by that he means that there is no servitude *altius non tollendi* implied in the legatee's favour. His reply, though often taken as a wide statement of principle, is in point of fact a particular reply[2] to a specific question on a point about legacies and servitudes, and we must be careful not to give it a greater scope than it has. We shall come back to it below.

The second question causes more difficulty. Does it make any difference if the heir raises the house in the estate or another house which he owns? In other words, is there an implied servitude *altius non tollendi* over any other house of the heir? This is quite subtle and it has been noticed since the time of the Gloss[3] that in the text as it stands at present, Marcellus does not reply. His reply may indeed have been cut out, or, as has also been noticed, his reply to the first question that there is no servitude over the estate house implies *a fortiori* the answer to this question. Hence there would be no need to state it specifically.

Whereas Beseler leaves the third question intact, merely changing *debet* to *debeat*,[4] Lenel wishes to cut it out.[5] He would strike out everything from *et de illo* to *debet*, so that the *sicut solet quaeri* part would then refer to 'what comes before'. He thinks the

---

[1] Mommsen, *Stereotype Digest*, 144 n. 18; Lenel, 39 (1918) *ZSS* 164 n. 2.
[2] Note the *alias*. [3] Gl. *binas, ad h. l.*
[4] 56 (1936) *ZSS* 85 ff. (in a study of *non semper*).
[5] 39 (1918) *ZSS* 164 ff. Followed by Kreller, *Deutsche Landesreferate*, 12.

question is definitely interpolated because no reply is given to it. Formal indications are the indicative *debet*; the use of *per alienas aedes* to describe a house in the ownership of the heir, whether the *aedes hereditariae* or *aedes propriae*; *ad eam rem* to refer to what must be a piece of land; *legatur* instead of *legata est*.

The fact that no reply is given cannot be decisive. This text has been so heavily abbreviated by the compilers that we may assume that the answer has been cut out. When Beseler does not react violently to the formal flaws pointed out by Lenel, lesser mortals should be wary. There has, however, been interference—the *ad eam rem* is odd; *debet* could be parataxis but is probably wrong; *legatur*, though perhaps strange, cannot be decisive on its own. The part *sicut . . . non potest* is, according to Lenel, to be connected directly with what goes before: the questioner sees the question whether the heir can block the legatee's lights as analogous with the question whether he can refuse the fructuary necessary access. But Lenel does not take any account of the second (admittedly minor) question which has come in between. If *sicut . . . non potest* were left standing by itself, it would be awkward and would create more problems than it solves.

What looks like Lenel's major objection on form, the *alienas* point, is more important and conceals a matter of substance. Lenel objects to *alienas* because he thinks that the question is whether the heir has to provide access through a house in his ownership. For that purpose *alienas* would be objectionable. If, however, *per alienas aedes* were taken in the natural way as 'through someone else's house', Gaurus would ask whether the heir must see to providing access to the subject of the legacy through a third party's house. In the original text, Gaurus would have been talking about a legacy *per damnationem* and the formally objectionable elements could be attributed to the compiler's activities in cutting out the details.

The fact that no other text discusses just this point would not in itself be decisive against holding the text genuine. There is a series of questions. Must the heir provide access for the fructuary over the estate land? Must he provide it over any other land which he owns? Must he provide it over another legatee's land? Must he provide it over a third party's land? However, although in theory the last looks as viable a question as any other, in practice it is not, since it is hard to contrive any but the most artificial set of facts in which the matter could be raised. Of course, Marcellus could have given just such a reply, but Lenel is right to be suspicious of the question. Gaurus may rather have put the question about access through a fellow legatee's land, the present text being merely a compilatorial version of what he said.

After having given his reply to the first question, viz. that no servitude is owed by the estate house to the legatee, Marcellus adds that the same is to be said, *si alteri aedes alteri aliarum usum fructum legaverit*. Mommsen,[1] referring to 7. 1. 30, wished to emend *aliarum* to *alterarum* and Lenel[2] was not averse to the suggestion. The reference to 7. 1. 30 is of doubtful relevance, but they may be right. Anyway Marcellus is talking about the situation where someone bequeaths one house to A and the usufruct in the other to B. The question is whether A owes a servitude *altius non tollendi* to B. Marcellus says he does not.

At first sight it is not clear why Marcellus draws this parallel. Beseler indeed changes the text so that Marcellus says *idem dicendum est, si usum fructum earum legaverit*.[3] No change is required and Marcellus' comparison is in point. Marcellus was faced with the problem of whether a legatee could claim an implied servitude *altius non tollendi* from the heir. The suggestion of these implied servitudes in favour of a legatee probably arose against the background of the fructuary's claims, which had been discussed in connection with testamentary usufructs. The fructuary could claim access, etc., and so could a simple legatee? However, the straightforward example of a fructuary claiming things like access or light from the heir in respect of property in the estate will not do as a parallel, for the simple reason that there is no question of a servitude in these circumstances. Marcellus takes the only fair parallel and that is whether or not the fructuary can successfully claim a servitude *altius non tollendi* from a fellow legatee. No other

[1] *Stereotype Digest*, 144 n. 19. See Mommsen, *Digest* 1, *editio maior*, 253, note to line 17.
[2] 39 *ZSS* 165 n. 2.
[3] 56 *ZSS* 86. On Beseler's correction see also below, 73.

case fits so well. The intermediate case of a fructuary claiming
access or light from a piece of land belonging to the heir but not
part of the testator's estate falls short, because again there is no
possibility of a servitude, the heir owning both pieces of land.
Likewise, the matter of a possible servitude over a complete
outsider's piece of land—the very doubtful case which comes up in
the third question as it is framed at present—would go too far
because there would be no relationship at all between the fructuary
and the person over whose land he sought the servitude. The
nearest to a true analogy is the situation which Marcellus envisages.
In both there is some kind of relationship, between the legatee and
the heir on the one hand, and between the fructuary and a co-
legatee on the other; but in both the ownership of the relevant
pieces of land is in separate hands and so the question of a servitude arises. Marcellus' example is the most appropriate.

A somewhat similar situation is found in another text of
Marcellus, 33. 2. 15. 1 which must be considered with 30. 44. 9.

Marcellus (13 digestorum) qui duos fundos habebat, unum legavit
et alterius fundi usum fructum alii legavit: quaero si fructuarius ad
fundum aliunde viam non habeat quam per illum fundum qui legatus
est, an fructuario servitus debeatur. respondit, quemadmodum, si in
hereditate esset fundus, per quem fructuario potest praestari via,
secundum voluntatem defuncti videtur id exigere ab herede, ita et in
hac specie non aliter concedendum esse legatario fundum vindicare,
nisi prius ius transeundi usufructuario praestet, ut haec forma in agris
servetur, quae vivo testatore optinuerit, sive donec usus fructus per-
manet sive dum ad suam proprietatem redierit.

30. 44. 9 Ulpian (22 ad Sabinum) si duos fundos habens testator
alterius mihi usum fructum, alterum Titio leget, aditum mihi legatarius
non debebit: sed heres cogitur redimere aditum et praestare.

In both texts[1] a testator bequeaths one *fundus* to A and the
usufruct in another to B. In 33. 2. 15. 1 Marcellus is asked
whether a servitude is owed to B when he cannot reach the subjects
of the usufruct except over A's *fundus*. If the questioner means by
that to ask whether the legatee owes a servitude to the fructuary,
that is a loose formulation since there can be no servitude to a

---

[1] Grosso, 5 (1939) *SDHI* 483 ff.; see also Astolfi, 23 (1957) *SDHI* 345 with
refs.

fructuary. Marcellus' reply is that just as B can demand a right of way from the heir over land in the estate, so A is not to be allowed to claim his *fundus* unless he has first made a *ius transeundi* available to the fructuary B. There is no way of telling the type of legacy of the usufruct, but depending on that factor B would be able to use either his *vindicatio* or his *actio ex testamento* to force the heir to secure the necessary access by interposing an *exceptio* to A's *vindicatio* of the other *fundus*.

30. 44. 9 is quite different. Ulpian says that A will not owe *aditus* to B but that the heir is obliged to purchase it from A and make it available to B. Strictly speaking Ulpian's denial of a servitude being owed by A to B does not clash with what is said in 33. 2. 15. 1. Grosso goes further and says that any difference between the texts is to be accounted for by the fact that the legacy of the usufruct is *per vindicationem* in 33. 2. 15. 1 and *per damnationem* in 30. 44. 9 so that in the latter all the obligations are on the heir while in the former it is A who actually owes the servitude, the heir being no more than a passive intermediary. Grosso's explanation is untenable. One of the differences between the texts is, however, almost certainly to be accounted for by saying that in 33. 2. 15. 1 A is a legatee *per vindicationem*—the text makes this plain—while in 30. 44. 9, A is a legatee *per damnationem*. Hence in the first case, A as owner can create a servitude himself, whereas in the second case as long as the heir has not transferred the *fundus* no servitude can be created.

So much is likely, but the fundamental problem remains and it seems to be insoluble on the texts as they stand. As far as can be seen, in 33. 2. 15. 1 the heir can oblige A to create a *ius transeundi* without A being paid for it. In 30. 44. 9, the heir purchases the *aditus*. This raises difficulties. It cannot have been the case that it was at A's discretion whether to make the *aditus* available because then he could have held the heir up to ransom since the usufruct would have been worth nothing without access. A could simply have charged the value of the land, for that is in effect what the access is worth. On the other hand, if A is obliged to grant access, how and by whom could a price be assessed? Anyway there seems no reason for the legatee *per damnationem* to be paid if the legatee *per vindicationem* is not. What one would have expected would be that the heir would withhold the access when transferring his *fundus* to A.

After all, the case is not far different from the one where land is bequeathed to a legatee but the heir is left two cottages inaccessible except over it. There, as we saw in 8. 5. 20 pr., Scaevola thought that access had to be given. The present case differs only in that for a certain length of time someone has a usufruct; eventually the heir or his successor will have full enjoyment and then the cases become identical, the heir requiring a servitude. For that reason, we should be slow to think of the *aditus* as anything less than a servitude. The reply is not specific and indeed the end, which is rightly regarded as more or less suspicious,[1] suggests that the right is limited in time. Although the right will lie in the fructuary's favour for only so long as the usufruct lasts, for the reasons indicated I incline to the view that the legatee will have to give a servitude with no agreement for terminating it.

The only very tentative observation to be made on 30. 44. 9 is that, though we have assumed it so far, Ulpian does not say anything about the subjects of the usufruct being inaccessible except through the other legatee's land. If they were not inaccessible, it would be quite reasonable to hold that no servitude is to be implied. The same applies to 33. 3. 1 where Julian declined to imply a servitude. The most probable solution for 30. 44. 9 would then be to say that *sed heres* to the end is spurious and may just possibly replace a discussion of how, if he wishes an inessential servitude, the fructuary will have to have it created by the heir. There could be no question of forcing the heir to obtain one.

Though there are these problems, they give no reason to doubt that in 8. 2. 10 Marcellus was in favour of the fructuary's claim to necessary access over a fellow legatee's land and that Ulpian agreed with this. Marcellus' decision in the case of access is different from his decision in the case of light where he is not in favour of implying a servitude in the fructuary's favour.

Marcellus now goes on to develop an argument from access. Before his argument is considered, the problem of access and the

---

[1] *Ind. Itp.*

fructuary's rights against the heir must be examined more widely in the sequence of texts 7. 6. 1. 1–4.

The Owner and the Fructuary's Right to Access

7. 6. 1. 1 Ulpian (18 ad Sabinum) usus fructus legatus adminiculis eget, sine quibus uti frui quis non potest: et ideo si usus fructus legetur, necesse est tamen ut sequatur eum aditus, usque adeo, ut, si quis usum fructum loci leget ita, ne heres cogatur viam praestare, inutiliter hoc adiectum videatur: item si usu fructu legato iter ademptum sit, inutilis est ademptio, quia semper sequitur usum fructum. 2. sed si usus fructus sit legatus, ad quem aditus non est per hereditarium fundum, ex testamento utique agendo fructuarius consequetur, ut cum aditu sibi praestetur usus fructus. 3. utrum autem aditus tantum et iter an vero et via debeatur fructuario legato ei usu fructu, Pomponius libro quinto dubitat: et recte putat, prout usus fructus perceptio desiderat, hoc ei praestandum. 4. sed an et alias utilitates et servitutes ei heres praestare debeat, puta luminum et aquarum, an vero non? et puto eas solas praestare compellendum sine quibus omnino uti non potest: sed si cum aliquo incommodo utatur, non esse praestandas.

This group of texts comes from Ulpian's discussion of the actions available to a legatee fructuary against the heir,[1] but the compilers have cut out all references to the different kinds of legacy.[2] Thus although in its place in the Digest the text looks as though it has to do with the fructuary's real action, it was probably as much concerned with actions on the will, as can be seen, for instance, in 7. 6. 1. 2. The matter of access was first settled for usufructs set up by will and the principles were transferred to usufruct established by *in iure cessio*.[3]

In 1. 1 Ulpian takes the simplest case and holds that where the usufruct of a house or land is bequeathed, the heir has to allow the fructuary access to it. This is not a matter of a servitude since the heir owns the subject of the usufruct. It is just a matter of the scope of the usufruct itself—there can be no *uti frui* without access and so the heir must provide it. In his essay on *et* (*atque*) *ideo* Beseler points out that our text has been revised and he provides a

---

[1] See above, 59.

[2] Lenel, *Pal.* 2, 1075. Cf. Lenel, *Das Sabinussystem*, 42 ff. The topic is dealt with in Pomponius 5 *ad Sabinum* and Paul 3 *ad Sabinum*. Cf. Lenel, *Pal.* 2, 98 and *Pal.* 1, 1258 respectively.

[3] Cf. V.F. 54.

version which restores references to a legacy *per damnationem*, but
leaves the point of the text undisturbed.[1]

In 1. 2 Ulpian takes the case where the *aditus* is not to be
through the *hereditarius fundus*, and the formulation probably
means that the *aditus* is to be over another *fundus* in the ownership
of the heir. Ulpian says that the fructuary can obtain the access
from the heir by suing *ex testamento*. Beseler[2] indicates that he
thinks that the text needs renovation though he does not say how:
probably he would bring out that the legacy was *per damnationem*
as is to be gathered from the words *ex testamento*. Again we have
no reason to assume any major change to the substance.

The next text, 1. 3, goes a stage further with Pomponius' doubts
about whether anything more than just *aditus* and *iter* should be
given, viz. something corresponding to *via*. Ulpian thought
Pomponius was correct to say it depended on the circumstances.
Beseler[3] says the later part of the text has been remodelled but
whether he regards it as altered in substance is not to be divined.
Substantial as opposed to formal alteration appears unlikely, since
the decision is given in rather too hesitant a form to make a good
interpolation. If it is genuine, Pomponius and Ulpian were prepared to extend the rights of the fructuary beyond mere *aditus* if
something more, like a right of *via*, was required for the operation
of the usufruct.

In 1. 4 leaving behind mere matters of access, Ulpian asks
whether or not the heir should provide other *utilitates et servitutes*,
for example lights and water. His hesitant reply is to the effect that
the heir is to be compelled to provide only those without which the
fructuary cannot use the usufruct at all. If he can use it, though
with some inconvenience, the *utilitates et servitutes* are not to be
provided.

Beseler would leave nothing of the text.[4] Grosso brackets *et
servitutes* and thinks the rest has been extensively altered.[5] So also
Bretone[6] who will not go as far as Beseler. The principal concern of
the Italians is that *servitutes* suggests that someone thought of the

[1] 45 (1925) *ZSS* 460.   [2] Loc. cit.
[3] 57 (1937) *ZSS* 30.   [4] 45 *ZSS* 460.
[5] *Usufrutto*, 200 ff. Followed by Kaser, *R.P.R.* 2, 220 n. 15.
[6] *La nozione romana di usufrutto* 2 (Naples, 1967), 42 n. 45.

fructuary as having a servitude over the portion of the estate in which he had no usufruct. This would be unclassical. It could, on the other hand, be a gloss or the result of abbreviation;[1] it is hardly enough by itself to cast grave doubt on the rest of the text. Presumably Beseler took exception to the question form, and perhaps to the indicative *potest*—but this latter usage is found in apparently classical texts. Strongly in favour of the classicality of the text is *puto* which is not a compilatorial word. The parts after it are correctly put into the accusative and infinitive. Formally the text looks quite sound.

Ulpian's reply is not easy to interpret. Grosso objects to it because he thinks that Ulpian should take a 'harder' line and bring out a strong contrast between access and light, allowing the fructuary the former but not the latter. In Grosso's view Ulpian's reply has been toned down by the compilers in the same way as they introduced moderation by interpolations in 7. 1. 30 and 8. 2. 10. However, the former is scarcely interpolated; there is no relevant interpolation in 8. 2. 10. Grosso also fails to notice Julian's decision in 43. 25. 1. 4. Ulpian's decision here is capable of an interpretation in line with those of Marcellus and Julian. What he says is that the fructuary can claim from the heir only those advantages which are essential to the operation of the usufruct but not any which merely serve to avoid inconvenience. In concrete terms this would mean that the fructuary can claim as much light as is necessary for the operation of his usufruct but no more. This is precisely what Paul reports Marcellus as saying in 7. 1. 30. Julian's view may or may not have been more favourable to the fructuary but at any rate it goes in the same direction as Ulpian's here. We should expect this since Ulpian reports Julian in 43. 25. 1. 4 with no sign of disagreement.

---

[1] Lenel puts 7. 6. 1 pr.-4 under the heading *De servitutibus quae usu fructu legato debentur. Pal.* 2, 1075. In his review of Lenel's *Palingenesia*, 33 (1891) *Kritische Vierteljahresschrift* 481 at 573, Kipp criticized this and said the passage would be better as part of Lenel's earlier section *De cautione usufructuaria et iure proprietarii*, Ulpian, nos. 2582–8. Lenel thought this 'less probable'. *Das Sabinussystem*, 43. There is something to be said for Kipp's suggestion since only 7. 6. 1 pr. definitely concerns servitudes. Yet, much may have been cut out including talk of possible servitudes from other legatees. The *servitutes* in 7. 6. 1. 4 may refer to something like that.

There is one final observation to be made before resuming the struggle with 8. 2. 10. We have clarified the scope of 7. 1. 30 and said that there is no reason to suppose interpolation. What must be noted further is that even were there interpolation of the last part of 7. 1. 30 and the last part of 8. 2. 10, the purpose of the interpolations would be different. 7. 1. 30 deals with the rights of the fructuary against the heir. 8. 2. 10 purports to say that the heir cannot block the lights of the legatee's house entirely but must leave enough light for everyday purposes.

The only part of 8. 2. 10 which corresponds to 7. 1. 30 is *habitare autem potest et aedibus obscuratis.* It cannot be the earlier *idem dicendum est . . . legaverit,* because that deals with the different matter of the legacy of one house to A and the usufruct in another to B.[1] Beseler saw this and changed that text to *idem dicendum est, si usum fructum earum legaverit.*[2] From the opposite point of view, Kreller wished to read 7. 1. 30 in the light of 8. 2. 10 and so to gloss 7. 1. 30 as having to do with the case where a man leaves two houses to A and the usufruct in one of them to B![3] Neither approach is correct. Both 8. 2. 10 and 7. 1. 30 should be taken as they stand. In 7. 1. 30 Paul preserves a record of part of Marcellus' discussion which the compilers almost entirely cut away.

An attempt can now be made to reconstruct the sense of 8. 2. 10, though it has been so severely shortened that precise restoration is not possible. The general outline may none the less be discerned. As was noted above,[4] Marcellus starts by saying that the heir can block the legatee's lights and likewise a fellow legatee can block a legatee fructuary's lights. By this Marcellus means that in neither case is a servitude *altius non tollendi* implied. In a part of the text which has been removed, it was remarked that in a similar situation the heir is bound to try to ensure that a legatee gives necessary access to the fructuary.[5] On this analogy, the objection was made, the legatee should be burdened with a servitude of lights in favour of the fructuary. From *non autem semper* onwards we have the gist of Marcellus' reply: the argument from *iter* is not

---

[1] Hence 7. 1. 30 can have no value for emendation of this part of 8. 2. 10 though Mommsen used it for that purpose. See above, 66.

[2] 56 *ZSS* 86.   [3] *Deutsche Landesreferate,* 12 n. 2.

[4] At 64.   [5] Cf. Marcellus, 33. 2. 15. 1 and Ulpian, 30. 44. 9.

always valid because, while there is no legacy of the fruit without access, you can actually live in a darkened house. This is a matter of principle and to illustrate it Marcellus goes back to the simple case of the fructuary against the heir, since that will be decisive of the more complicated case: if the fructuary cannot force the owner-heir to refrain from raising his house at all, then *a fortiori* he cannot succeed with the legatee. The sentence beginning *ceterum usu fructu* represents a doubtless abridged version of what Marcellus said. It was to the effect that the fructuary could demand access from the heir, this being implied in the usufruct which would be unworkable without it, just in the same way as a servitude of *haustus* necessarily implies one of *iter* to the source of the water. None the less, Marcellus went on in a section which has been cut out but which is referred to by Paul in 7. 1. 30, the fructuary cannot demand that the heir should not build at all—which would be the effect of a right of light corresponding to a servitude *altius non tollendi* in the same way as the fructuary's *aditus* corresponds to the servitude *iter*. The heir is free to build but—here we come to *quod usque adeo — habeant* in 7. 1. 30—he cannot block the fructuary's light completely and has to leave enough light for ordinary everyday purposes. Marcellus was merely stating what followed from the ordinary principles of usufruct.[1]

From this point conjecture becomes harder. By this argument, Marcellus has justified his decision that there can be no substance in the fructuary's claim to a servitude *altius non tollendi* over a fellow legatee's land. He cannot demand the equivalent from the heir himself and so he cannot expect it from the legatee. On this basis, all that the fructuary can require of the heir is that he ensure that the legatee does not deprive him of enough light to live in his house. Since Marcellus has already (*idem dicendum est . . .*) put this case of the fructuary against his fellow legatee on the same level as the initial case of the legatee against the heir, he may have returned now to this initial case and remarked that a like decision is to be given there. That is what we find in the last sentence of 8. 2. 10.

This last sentence may have stood much as it stands now and Marcellus may have given a full version of his final decision on the

---

[1] Cf. Julian, 43. 25. 1. 4 and Ulpian, 7. 6. 1. 4.

first question. On the other hand, he may merely have said something like *idem dicendum est* . . . with a reference to the initial problem, but in effect leaving the reader to find his decision from the usufruct case. It is impossible to tell, but if he did so, this might explain certain oddities in the last sentence. The compilers of the title 8. 2 were not interested in the usufruct business; what they wanted was the legacy decision and so what they may have done is merely to insert *legatas* into Marcellus' formulation of the rights of the fructuary. That would account for the close resemblance of the two sentences in 7. 1. 30 and 8. 2. 10 which are none the less crucially different. That assumption would also explain the *habitantibus* to which both Pernice[1] and Riccobono[2] object. Speaking of 8. 2. 10 Pernice says that we have heard nothing of these *habitantes* so far and he weakly concludes that an interpolator was thinking of tenants such as those mentioned in 19. 2. 25. 2. Riccobono says that *habitantibus* appears where we should expect *legatario* in 8. 2. 10 but he merely notes critically the *habitantibus* *sufficit* of 7. 1. 30. No criticism can be brought against *habitantibus* in 7. 1. 30—there has been no mention of anyone else and the verb seems quite suitable for referring to people occupying a house under a usufruct. In 8. 2. 10, as we now have it, the word is perhaps slightly out of place—not very seriously, but a little. If this part of the text originally referred to usufruct, and the compilers have altered it by interpolating *legatas*, *habitantibus* may not be objectionable since the illustration may have referred, as in 7. 1. 30, to more than one occupier of the house; *habitantibus* would certainly not be standing in place of *legatario*. On the other hand use of the vaguer word *habitantibus* may be deliberate—otherwise the case of the legatee's wife or children would not strictly speaking be covered.

There are certain conclusions to be drawn. The very real problems of 8. 2. 10 are not to be solved by supposing interpolation, but rather one has to be aware of the ruthless abridgement which the passage has suffered at the hands of the compilers. If the reconstruction above is along the right lines, the text represents merely a fragmented version of Marcellus' reply to the first question. His answers to the second and third have been cut away.

[1] *Labeo* 2 1, 65 n. 4.   [2] 21 *RISG* 397 n. 1.

Likewise all allusions to the types of legacy and types of actions have vanished. The text is about whether or not there is an implied servitude of light over land in the estate and in favour of the legatee. Hence one cannot object that, if it were true, as I argue, that a man could not block his neighbour's lights, the present text would not have raised a valid point. The present text is asking whether the heir can build at all—which he could not if there were such a servitude. When Marcellus replies that the heir can undoubtedly build and block the legatee's lights, then that is correct because there is no servitude; only it is subject to the proviso which duly appears, though much later, that he cannot block the legatee's lights completely. The legatee, in other words, turns out to be in no better a position than anyone else. Yet Gaurus' inquiries were legitimate, because texts such as 8. 5. 20 pr. and 33. 3. 1 indicate that early classical jurists were concerned with similar problems of implied servitudes.

III.   The next text in the Digest, 8. 2. 11 is hard to explain in terms of a classical law which knew no restrictions on the freedom of an owner to build.

Ulpian (1 de officio consulis) qui luminibus vicinorum officere aliudve quid facere contra commodum eorum vellet, sciet se formam ac statum antiquorum aedificiorum custodire debere. 1. si inter te et vicinum tuum non convenit, ad quam altitudinem extolli aedificia, quae facere instituisti, oporteat, arbitrum accipere poteris.

It is convenient to start with 11. 1. This tells us that if you do not agree with your neighbour about how high it is right for you to raise the building which you have started to construct, you will be able to have an arbiter.

If an owner was free to build in classical law, there should be no thought of him having to agree a height with his neighbour: in the absence of a servitude he can do what he likes. This embarrassing text has been largely ignored. One way out[1] would be to say that Ulpian is supposing a case where a servitude *altius non tollendi* has been constituted. This servitude would contain some limit or

---

[1] Taken, I think, by A. dell'Oro, *I 'Libri de Officio' nella giurisprudenza romana* (Milan, 1960), 35 ff. His suggestion on the palingenesia of the text does not convince.

other, perhaps formulated simply as *ne luminibus officiatur*; the job of the arbiter would be to decide whether or not the proposed building would infringe the limit. This would be a perfectly acceptable role for the arbiter; the real objection is that the theory requires us to read into the text an element which is not mentioned, the existence of a servitude. Of course a servitude could have been mentioned in the original version and have been left to be implied from the surrounding context in the Digest, but the fact remains that there is no evidence for a servitude. Indeed most scholars have accepted that the text is awkward just because no servitude is envisaged.

Buckland[1] treats 11. 1 as evidence for seeing the so-called servitude *altius tollendi* as a counter-servitude allowing partial release, apparently from a pre-existing servitude *altius non tollendi*. I cannot understand quite what he means here.

Biondi at least faces up to the issue. 'Given that the owner can build freely, both the nomination of an arbiter and the determination by him of a *modus altitudinis* are inconceivable for the classical jurists.'[2] Logically enough Biondi decides that 11. 1 is interpolated to take account of the Justinianic position as he conceives it, but he hesitates to reconstruct the text and declines to follow an 'audacious critic' who might argue that the reference to the arbiter is interpolated and that the text originally affirmed the neighbour's right to build *in infinitum*.[3]

Biondi was correct not to take that course. The text comes from the first book of Ulpian *de officio consulis*, a work composed in Caracalla's reign.[4] Lenel puts our text under the rubric *de iudice arbitrove dando*[5] and there are three other texts[6] all referring to *arbitri* which back him up. The reference to the arbiter cannot be interpolated because it is impossible seriously to contend that the compilers not only wrote a text about an arbiter but attributed it to Ulpian and to the correct book of this minor work. An arbiter implies a dispute to resolve; fragment 1 provides a suitable one in any legal system where a man can put up a building subject only to

---

[1] *Textbook*, 264 n. 11.   [2] *Cat.* 53.   [3] *Cat.* 53 ff.
[4] Lenel, *Pal.* 2, 951 n. 1. Hence of similar date to C. 3. 34. 1.
[5] *Pal.* 2, 951.   [6] 5. 1. 82; 35. 1. 50; 42. 5. 27.

the limitation that he must leave his neighbour a reasonable amount of light: A starts to build but he and his neighbour B cannot agree how high a building would leave B with less than the reasonable amount of light. A can submit the matter to an arbiter who will decide for the parties. That is the simplest construction of what the text tells us. Adherents to the orthodox doctrine must assume that the text is interpolated; but there is nothing in the form of the text to justify suspicion and no grounds other than *a priori* ones for doubting that it is genuine.

The principium of the text is also interesting and no more than 11. 1 can it be part of the orthodox picture of the classical law. Accordingly it is rejected as spurious by most writers.[1] Since the fundamental problem with this text is similar to that with 11. 1 it is hard to understand how scholars can consistently reject the principium but remain silent on 11. 1. It may be that they would argue that 11. 1 referred originally to a servitude. Be that as it may, the problems are not dissimilar.

Most writers are content to follow Riccobono who relies on the clash of moods *vellet–sciet* and the use of the third person as revealing the style of the chancellery and the legislative character of the content. However, it is notorious that in matters of style the works *de officiis* are a law unto themselves and that 'criticism based on stylistic grounds must therefore be applied to the surviving texts with great caution'.[2] This is not to deny that there may have been some interference—for example *aliudve quid facere* looks like an insertion—but these grounds alone scarcely justify rejecting the text.

Riccobono goes much further and claims that the section 'evidently' contains a translation of a bit from the constitution of Zeno preserved as C. 8. 10. 12. 1a. The piece in question is:

προστάττομεν τοὺς τὰς ἰδίας οἰκίας ἀνανεοῦντας τὸ ἀρχαῖον σχῆμα μηδαμῶς παρεξιέναι, ὥστε μὴ τοὺς οἰκοδομοῦντας ἀφαιρεῖσθαι φῶτα ἢ ἄποψιν τῶν γειτόνων παρὰ τὸ πάλαι καθεστηκός.

The standard Latin translation gives perhaps an even better basis for assessing the similarities:

[1] See *Ind. Itp.* and Solazzi, *Specie*, 104 ff.; also below, 116.
[2] Schulz, *Roman Legal Science*, 242 ff. and refs.

. . . cum praecipiat, ut qui aedes suas renovant nequaquam veterem formam excedant, ne aedificantes lumina vel prospectum vicinorum contra priorem statum auferant . . .

This piece and 8. 2. 11 pr. are similar, but the most superficial comparison also reveals that there are enough differences to make it rash to claim that the Digest text derives from the other. Both are on the same theme; certain similarities inevitably follow. It would be rather strange if the Digest commissioners actually chose to reproduce these words of Zeno since he is merely reporting a provision of Leo and may well be paraphrasing rather than quoting exactly. Anyway, if 11 pr. is meant to have been written by Byzantines to expound the Byzantine position, the writers were curiously slipshod since they omitted to mention, what must surely have been the leading ordinance, that provided a space of 12 feet was left between the houses the builder could build as high as he wished —even when he was renewing an old house.[1] While 11 pr. may be seen as a classical text being adapted (not wholly successfully) to the new regime, it can hardly be regarded as the best description which the compilers could devise of that new regime.

We are thrown back on the assumption that 11 pr. is in essence classical. Karlowa saw as much and concluded that in certain circumstances an owner had less than unrestricted freedom to build even under classical and pre-classical law.[2] Without adopting his explanation of the classical law, we can and should agree with him that 11 pr. is a further indication that the classical owner was not entirely unfettered in this matter.

It is worth pausing briefly to look at 8. 2. 9, *h.t.* 10 and *h.t.* 11 as a group. They all come in the regular order of excerpting; none has been displaced. Were Lenel's proposed palingenesia of 8. 2. 31 correct, it would originally have come between 9 and 10, but for once Lenel has nodded and Paul's text is best left in its present position in the Sabinian Mass.[3] 9 then marks the end of the section comprising the texts *ad edictum* excerpted jointly.

---

[1] C. 8. 10. 12. 2. [2] *Rechtsgeschichte* 2, 530 ff.

[3] Lenel assigns 8. 2. 31 to Paul's commentary on *operis novi nuntiatio. Pal.* 1, 1055 and n. 2. *E.P.* 370 n. 9. This is incorrect, since Paul 48 fin. *ad edictum* which contains the *operis novi nuntiatio* portion was assigned to the Edictal Committee. Cf. Krüger's version of Bluhme's table, no. 121 in the *Stereotype*

Since it comes in its correct position 9 was picked out for use in this title during the initial work of reading through the classical books.[1] Now it is useful in the title on servitudes only in something like its present form and so it had reached more or less that form by the time it had been added to the bundle of texts destined to make up this title. That means that already at this stage the compilers were taking as their basic statement of the law the notion that an owner can build freely. It also suggests that for some reason or other no statement of such a principle was found in the classical authors.

10 and 11 are out of line with 9. No theory can avoid that fact. Hitherto the argument has always been that 9 states the classical law and is therefore inconsistent with 10 and 11 which give Justinianic modifications of it. Once we appreciate that 9 represents the views of the compilers, the argument is reversed and we must be prepared to look on 10 and 11 as inconsistent with 9 because they reflect classical opinions while 9 is Byzantine. If recent work[2] on the compilation of the Digest is correct, then 9 was excerpted by C and his helpers while 10 was excerpted by D, but that does not of itself explain how 9 and 10 come to take these rather differing approaches. Anyway 9 and 11 which are also inconsistent should have both been part of C's assignment.[3]

Digest. Paul 48 init. *ad edictum* was assigned to the Sabinian Committee. Bluhme's table, no. 5. 8. 2. 31 is from Paul 48 *ad edictum* and is from the Sabinian Mass. One would have to suppose the strangest coincidence if one wished to argue that it was from the Edictal Mass and had been moved. Hence Lenel's palingenesia is virtually impossible and anyway there is nothing in the text to back it up. It is better to assume that the text is from Paul on the *cautio legatorum servandorum causa*, a topic dealt with in book 48 init. This obviates the problem of the masses. In 8. 2. 31 Paul was not talking about servitudes, but about legacies. Beseler saw as much, but his reconstruction of the fragment and its reallocation to book 47 are unjustified. However, his deletion of (the linguistically unacceptable) *servitutemque praestaret* is correct. 43 (1923) *ZSS* 540. To be precise, Paul was concerned with the problems of a negative legacy, the *cautio* being designed for positive legacies. Cf. *dari fierive* and *detur vel fiat* in 36. 3. 1 pr., Ulpian 79 *ad edictum*. See Lenel, *E.P.* 539. The words *servitutemque praestaret* were inserted to make the text more applicable to its place in a servitude title. See also 8. 4. 16, Gaius 2 *rerum cottidianarum* and J. 2. 3. 4, discussed briefly above at 25 n. 2. The matter cannot be fully investigated here.

[1] On the palingenesia see above, 8 ff.
[2] Honoré, Rodger, 87 (1970) *ZSS* 246.
[3] Honoré, Rodger, 87 *ZSS* 299 and 301.

Since someone went to the trouble of moving and reshaping 9,
we may think that the compilers were sufficiently wide awake to
have been aware of what they were doing. If so, they may have
seen 10 and 11, not as subverting their own rule, but as embodying
qualifications of that rule in specific cases. Thus they would hold
that despite the general notion of freedom to build, no heir should
block a legatee's light entirely—the relationship between them
would make any such qualification defensible. Hence 10 could be
admitted. As for 11, Byzantine legislation dealt with long-existing
buildings as a special case and so 11 pr. could be referred to that
statute. Where 11. 1 comes into the Justinianic system is not so
clear to me as most scholars seem to find it, but the compilers may
have known what they thought they meant by it.

Such at least would be the most charitable interpretation which
one could put on the confusion in this set of texts. Worst of all
would be to say that not only is 9 Justinianic but 10 and 11 have
been interpolated in the opposite direction. The compilers may
have been bad, but they were usually better than that. One must
choose between 9 on the one side and 10 and 11 on the other. For
all the reasons outlined above I unhesitatingly choose 9 for the
Justinianic law, 10 and 11 for the classical law.

IV.   8. 2. 27. 1 is too ambiguous a text for anything to be founded
on it.

Pomponius (33 ad Sabinum) si in area communi aedificare velis,
socius prohibendi ius habet, quamvis tu aedificandi ius habeas a vicino
concessum quia invito socio in iure communi non habeas ius aedificandi.

Pomponius was writing about servitudes[1] in relation to common
ownership. Having discussed in the principium the actionability
of damage to other property of one *socius* arising from the common
property, and damage to the common property arising from other
property of one of the *socii*, Pomponius now states that even though
he has an *aedificandi ius* from a neighbour still one *socius* can be
prevented from building by his fellow *socius*.

---

[1] Lenel, *Pal.* 2, 144. On the entire fragment, Lenel compares 10. 3. 28,
Papinian, 7 *quaestionum*. For lit., see *Ind. Itp.* Add Grosso, *Studi Albertoni* 1,
476; Biondi, *Cat.* 310 and Solazzi, *Specie*, 127.

As a statement of law relating to co-ownership, it is unremarkable enough[1] but the nature of the neighbour's concession is not so clear. We can say with Bonfante, Grosso, and Solazzi that the neighbour had a servitude *altius non tollendi* over the common property and has waived his right to object, whether he has renounced his servitude or merely forgone his objection. Assuming the former leads to certain difficulties since the text suggests at least a renunciation to one owner, and, as Biondi pointed out,[2] it is not at all clear that this would be effective. On the other hand, the verb used is *concessum* which may refer to a mere agreement not to object. That could probably be made with one owner.

Attributing the neighbour's power here to a servitude *altius non tollendi* requires us yet again to assume one where none is mentioned. We may be dealing with an excision for the purposes of abbreviation. All that need be pointed out is that supposing a classical right to object removes the need for such fiddling with the text. The neighbour would have been able to intervene on the strength of his ownership, using an *actio negatoria*. That is enough to justify inclusion of the text in a section on servitudes. The neighbour has simply agreed, presumably for a money consideration, to allow the *socius* to build. But given all the uncertainties of this brief text no great weight can be placed on it.

8. 2. 41. 1 is not relevant:

Scaevola (1 responsorum) Lucius Titius aperto pariete domus suae, quatenus stillicidii rigor et tignorum protectus competebat, ianuam in publico aperuit: quaero, cum neque luminibus Publii Maevii vicini neque itineri vicini officeret neque stillicidium ne [stillicidio ne de— Mommsen] vicini domo cadat, an aliquam actionem Publius Maevius vicinus ad prohibendum haberet. respondi secundum ea quae proponerentur nullam habere.

The difficulty for commentators is that, although on the facts Scaevola says the neighbour cannot prevent Lucius Titius from constructing a door, none the less he seems to think that if it

---

[1] Though the disputes about the need for positive consent mean that suspicions have been cast on the end. Bonfante, *Scritti* 3, 414 ff.

[2] Biondi himself thought there was a Justinianic reference to his legal servitudes, but in Biondi's elaborate version they are inherently implausible. See Grosso, 5 (1939) *SDHI* 238, Book Review.

blocked the neighbour's lights or interfered with his *iter* or stillicide, Publius Maevius could prevent him. No servitude is mentioned and it is hard to introduce any since even one of Scaevola's questioners would be sinking to the depths of banality if he asked whether an action which did not breach the servitude could be prevented. Solazzi followed Biondi in holding the text interpolated.[1]

The solution has been obscured by a suggestion of interpolation made by Ferrini[2] who was apparently inspired by the following lines of Cuiacius:[3]

L. Titius aperto pariete domus suae januam in publico aperuit quatenus stillicidii rigor et tignorum protectus competebat, quatenus ambitum aedium Scaevola definiebat, auctore Cicerone: non est igitur egressus ambitum aedium in aperienda, neque vero potuit. . . .

Cuiacius goes on to say that the neighbour was objecting to an invasion of privacy since L. Titius would have a view into his house, but that he had no action on this account. Referring to Cuiacius, Ferrini asserted that the text is about *ambitus*. More than that, Ferrini argued that *in publico* had been interpolated for *in ambitum* to bring the text into line with the Byzantine building regulations.[4] In the course of the one book Biondi offered two different theories of how a reference to *ambitus* had been removed from this text: firstly[5] he proposed that *iter vicini* had been substituted for the classical *ambitus* and later[6] he took the same line as Ferrini. Grosso sided with Ferrini but considered that the words *neque luminibus Publii Maevii vicini* might be spurious.[7]

This train of thought is misconceived. The words *in publico* are not interpolated but give the key to the solution. Scaevola is discussing the edict *ne quid in loco publico*. So Ulpian says: *propter quod si quod forte opus in publico fiet, quod ad privati damnum redundet, prohibitorio interdicto potest conveniri. . . .*[8] As has been mentioned often already, this edict covered loss caused by blocking

---

[1] *Specie*, 79. Biondi referred the interpolation to his Justinianic system of legal servitudes.

[2] *Opere* 1, 439.   [3] *Obs.* 13, 27, i.e. *Opera* (Venice, 1758 edition) 3, 351.
[4] *Opere* 1, 440 n. 2.   [5] *Cat.* 50.   [6] *Cat.* 114.
[7] *Studi Albertoni* 1, 471 n. 40.
[8] 43. 8. 2. 2, Ulpian 68 *ad edictum*.

a neighbour's lights.[1] It also lay if people were hindered in going to and fro by some structure which made the road narrower or less convenient.[2] The reference to *stillicidium* is obscure and may be an insertion or the result of amalgamation, but interference with a neighbour's gutters could be annoying for him and almost certainly he would have a remedy if the nuisance was substantial.

Scaevola's reply does not reveal his thinking, and the mere fact that the various infringements did not occur is enough to justify his decision. Yet another point may be raised in the text. The description of the door *in publico* as being *quatenus stillicidii rigor et tignorum protectus competebat* is difficult to translate but seems to mean that the door, though *in publico*, was no further out than the line of the gutter and the beams.[3] Presumably no one could object to those, and the question may be whether any action could be raised about a door which was no more *in publico* than they. One is reminded of the person who claimed that his lights were being obstructed by a shade stretched on his neighbour's balcony. Ulpian held that an *interdictum utile* lay.[4] The form of Scaevola's reply does not reveal his thoughts on the matter.

It is not against this approach that Scaevola talks in terms of an *actio*. That is how the question is framed and Scaevola does not bother to rephrase it when no remedy is to be given anyway.

---

[1] 43. 8. 2. 14, Ulpian 68 *ad edictum.*

[2] 43. 8. 2. 32, Ulpian 68 *ad edictum.*

[3] *stillicidii rigor.* The *VIR* shows that *rigor* is a rare word in juristic texts. The *VIR* editors bracketing our text with 43. 12. 1. 5, Ulpian 68 *ad edictum* and 43. 13. 1. 3, Ulpian 68 *ad edictum* say that the meaning is *rigor cursus,* i.e. the line of the river. Forcellini also translates *il filo dell'acqua* and adds '*Sic* stillicidii rigor *apud* Scaev. ibid. 8. 2. 41. *est rectus flexus, quo naturaliter defluit.*' Although right for the other two passages, this meaning is wrong here. Better is the usage from a technical term of the *agrimensores*: '*rigor est quidquid inter duo signa veluti in modum lineae rectum perspicitur* . . . *nam quidquid in agro mensorii operis causa ad finem rectum fuerit rigor appellatur*: *quidquid ad horum imitationem in forma scribitur, linea appellatur.*' Balbus, *ad Celsum Expositio et Ratio Omnium Formarum,* Lachmann, *Die Schriften der römischen Feldmesser* 1, 98. Cf. Rudorff in *Feldmesser* 2 (Berlin, 1852), 432. For use with genitives, cf. *Feldmesser* 1, 287. 26, *in rigore limitis*; 303. 18 ff., *per rigorem vicinarum possessionum*; 319. 19, *collis rigorem sequeris.* Cuiacius has the correct meaning here. *Opera* 3, 234 and 6, 697. O. S. S. 1, 722 also appear to be on the right lines ('innerhalb der Grenzen'). Their rendering otherwise leaves much to be desired. In our passage the word refers to a straight line which would mark on the ground the distance of the gutters from the building.

[4] 43. 8. 2. 6. Ulpian 68 *ad edictum.*

Besides, despite suggestions to the contrary, the term *actio* could be used even in classical law to refer to an interdict.[1]

The palingenesia of 8. 2. 41 is no great hindrance to this interpretation. Lenel puts the text under the rubric *de servitutibus*,[2] probably rightly, though neither section of the text is directly on that subject. 41 pr. is concerned with the scope of a legacy of *habitatio*, the question being whether the heir has a right of passage through the subjects of the *habitatio* to an otherwise inaccessible house and garden which he had inherited. While allowing him access, Scaevola in passing remarks that there is no servitude. Seemingly that sort of a matter could find its way into a book on servitudes,[3] though one could argue that a more likely origin would be in a preceding section on usufruct and allied topics. Matters relating to public roads and their effect on servitudes crop up from time to time in servitude texts.[4] More especially Alfenus, when asked how a neighbour could be forced to remove a dung-heap which was making a wall damp, replied that if the heap had been made *in loco publico* an interdict could be used, if *in privato*, *de servitute agere oportere*.[5] When such questions of public land occurred, allusion would frequently be made to the appropriate remedy. So a place for 41. 1 also can be found in a servitude context. Admittedly in both instances the topics must have occurred more or less as side issues. There is nothing to prevent us saying that the principium is from a usufruct, 41. 1 from a servitude context.

For present purposes 41. 1 may be ignored since it does not deal with building on private land.

8. 5. 15 presents many difficulties for anyone trying to puzzle out its meaning, but even more for scholars who adhere to the orthodox view of lights.[6]

Ulpian (6 opinionum) altius aedes suas extollendo, ut luminibus domus [minoris annis viginti quinque vel] impuberis, cuius [curator

---

[1] Lenel, *E.P.* 477. [2] *Pal.* 2, 289.
[3] Cf. 8. 5. 2. 2, Ulpian 17 *ad edictum*. Lenel, *Pal.* 2, 517.
[4] e.g. 8. 1. 14. 2, Paul 15 *ad Sabinum*; 8. 2. 1 pr., Paul 21 *ad edictum*; 39. 3. 17. 2, Paul 15 *ad Plautium*.
[5] 8. 5. 17. 2, Alfenus 2 *digestorum*. Lenel, *Pal.* 1, 38. For certain difficulties, see refs. in Watson, *Property*, 177 n. 2.
[6] Solazzi, *Specie*, 73 n. 159 and refs.

vel] tutor erat, officiatur, efficit: quamvis hoc quoque nomine actione ipse heredesque teneantur, quia quod alium facientem prohibere ex officio necesse habuit, id ipse committere non debuit, tamen et adversus possidentem easdem aedes danda est impuberi [vel minori] actio, ut quod non iure factum est tollatur.

The parts in square brackets are generally agreed interpolations and since the matter is of no consequence for us we may concede that they are so. As it stands, the text says that if a tutor blocks his pupil's lights by building up his own house, although the tutor and his heirs are liable on this account also, viz. because he ought not himself to have done what it was his duty to prevent others from doing, nevertheless the *impubes* will be given an action even against the possessor of the same house, to remove what was done unlawfully. The paraphrase could be modified in certain ways, but most importantly the manuscript F reads *altius aedes tuas extollendo* which would mean that the tutor was not raising his own house. Nor is it clear to whom *possidentem* refers. Biondi and Solazzi assume that the reference is to some third-party possessor, but it could be to the tutor himself, at least if *tuas* is the correct reading. That interpretation would square with the earlier *hoc quoque nomine*, which might lead us to think that Ulpian is considering the concurrence of two actions. Even the nature of these actions is far from certain: the *actione* is usually taken (for example, by Solazzi) as being the *actio tutelae*; the palingenesia of the text[1] which places it in a section on servitudes would prompt the conclusion that the second action mentioned is something to do with servitudes. Yet why *danda est*? It may be because the defendant is a mere possessor. Nothing is certain and the text must be handled with due caution.

There is no explicit mention of a servitude and yet the tutor commits a wrong by blocking the pupil's lights. He thereby does something which it would be his duty to prevent another from doing—this implies that the tutor should take an action on his pupil's behalf against someone blocking his lights. Also the pupil has an action to remove *quod non iure factum est*. There is not a hint of a servitude. Of course mention of a servitude *altius non tollendi*

---

[1] Lenel, *Pal.* 2, 1012.

may have been cut out by the compilers—Biondi favours assuming this.[1] It is not plain why the compilers should have taken that step. For Boháček everything from *quia quod* to *tollatur* is to be rejected as alluding to Justinian's legal servitudes.[2] This excision was too much even for a strong interpolationist like Solazzi who is forced none the less to choose between the legal servitudes of Justinian's era and some vague administrative prohibition of Ulpian's time.

With this second suggestion Solazzi comes close to accepting what seems the simplest way out of the tangle: Ulpian assumes that blocking of lights can be unlawful, even without a servitude. The tutor blocks his pupil's lights and is liable on the *actio tutelae* for doing so when he would be bound to take action against anyone doing the same because such blocking is unlawful. The possessor of the house, whoever he is, must remove the offending structure—it offends, not because of any servitude but just because it blocks the pupil's lights to more than the permitted degree.

No attempt is made to disguise the fact that many questions about this text remain unanswered; but in this way one perplexing feature is eliminated.

We saw above[3] that 19. 2. 25. 2 furnishes no aid to the view that blocking is always lawful, and now we argue that it may weigh, however slightly, in favour of the argument being presented.[4]

According to Gaius a landlord is liable to his tenant if the room which he is leasing is darkened. If the next part is sound, Gaius adds that the tenant can abandon the lease and that if the landlord demands the rent some reduction must be made. The same is to be said if the landlord does not restore doors and windows which have fallen into excessive disrepair.

The first part down to *inquilino* is a quotation by Gaius from some other writer. Beseler would cross out *certe — habenda est.*

---

[1] *Scritti* 2, 638. The rest of his explanation is misguided.

[2] 46 (1939) *BIDR* 190 n. 96. These servitudes flourish in the literature but have only the most superficial roots in the texts. C. 8. 10. 12. 2b. See 82 n. 2.

[3] At 10 f., where the text is set out.

[4] See *Ind. Itp.* Add Beseler, 57 (1937) *ZSS* 44; 66 (1948) *ZSS* 355; Kreller, 66 (1948) *ZSS* 85 n. 132; G. Longo, *Ricerche romanistiche* (Milan, 1966), 526; T. Mayer-Maly, *Locatio Conductio* (Vienna, Munich, 1956), 153; Kaser, 74 (1957) *ZSS* 184 n. 121.

He thinks that *reputationis* can hardly be meant to refer to reduction in rent and any more general declaration that compensation will be made is too plain to require stating.[1] The language may be a bit too vague but we are on less sure footing if we say the classical law was very different—Beseler himself does not do so specifically —and even though G. Longo thinks we have to do with post-classical developments, quite a number of authorities accept the present version.[2] The matter is not critical for us.

The last sentence is relevant. It is deleted by both Longo and Mayer-Maly. This approach is useless because the sentence has *eadem intellegemus* typical of Gaius[3] and of no other writer; unless we posit an improbable *Gaiuskenner* among interpolators we must accept that this sentence was from the same pen as the first of the passage, though Beseler brackets *nimium*. The reason why these authors remove this last sentence is interesting: if one accepts that the blocking of the landlord's lights is something against which he could do nothing—unless take out a servitude—then his liability must simply be because the lease is no longer viable. The part *eadem intellegemus* looks as though it is putting his liability for non-repair of doors and windows on the same level as that for the loss of light. Yet he is liable because of his failure to remedy the defects in these when he could. On this basis Gaius is equating liability for something about which the defendant could do nothing with that for something which he could remedy. Hence the (unacceptable) deletions of Longo and Mayer-Maly.

Jörs and Kunkel manage to stomach the discrepancy merely by saying that unilateral repudiation of the contract was possible both in the case of breach by the other party, for example, non-payment of rent or non-repair of damage to the subjects of hire (citing the end of our text), and in any event where the party renouncing could point to impairment of his enjoyment under the contract

---

[1] *Beiträge* 5, 37. Professor Daube kindly informs me that in lectures delivered in Cambridge before the Second World War, he wondered if there was an allusion to the possibility that even (*quoque*) rent for a part already due might be adjusted when that period would not necessarily have been worth anything. Cf. 19. 2. 24. 4, Paul 34 *ad edictum*.

[2] e.g. Kaser and Jörs–Kunkel, *Römisches Privatrecht*, 238.

[3] Cf. G. 1. 72, 2. 107, 2. 183, 2. 233, 3. 45, 3. 101, 3. 114, 4. 135.

(citing the first part of our text)[1] Perhaps the German scholars are right; after all, the same remedy may be given in unlike cases. Yet there is a discrepancy which will be much reduced if a man could prevent excessive blocking of his lights, for then the landlord is liable for the results of a blocking which he should have prevented and which he may still be able to remove by appropriate action. That would put the decision on lights on roughly the same basis and make Gaius' parallel appropriate.

Other attacks on this conclusion could be made—for instance, we cannot be sure that the *eadem intellegemus* portion came side by side with the other in the original—but the text may be a straw in the wind pointing, however unsurely, in the desired direction.

The aim of this chapter was to suggest that excessive blocking of lights was unlawful in classical law. The main evidence to support that conclusion is 39. 2. 25 where Paul quotes Trebatius as giving a remedy on the *cautio damni infecti* in just such circumstances. This implies that blocking is unlawful. 8. 2. 11 also suggests a system where the builder had to pay some attention to his neighbour. 8. 2. 10 is seen to be an abbreviated version of a decision by Marcellus denying that an heir owes any servitude of light to a legatee under the same will; the latter is not in a special position and must simply be accorded the usual necessary minimum of light. Taken together, 39. 2. 25, 8. 2. 10, and 8. 2. 11 suggest that classical Roman law protected light and this conclusion is strengthened when we find that the compilers, who could not discover any statement that an owner was completely free to build, were obliged to manufacture the one which now stands as 8. 2. 9. Other fragments, 8. 2. 27. 1, 8. 5. 15, and 19. 2. 25. 2, all present aspects which would be easier to explain in such a system as we suppose, though none of them is otherwise inexplicable.

From all this it may be deduced that excessive blocking of light was unlawful. Such a deduction receives its strongest confirmation in the existence of the servitude *altius tollendi*. In the legal regime which the orthodox doctrine claims to detect, that servitude is out of place. And yet it existed. It falls easily into the proposed system and may be examined within that context.

[1] *Römisches Privatrecht*, 238.

3. FORMULAE AND ACTIONS

In the preceding chapters it has been asserted that an owner had a right to a reasonable amount of light. Since both the concept of a reasonable minimum amount of light and the concept of excessive blocking of light have been and will be mentioned frequently, it is proper to admit that the precise meaning of these terms cannot be ascertained. In 8. 2. 10 a reasonable amount of light is what is sufficient for the everyday requirements of the inhabitants. That is vague, as are all statements using words like large, small, medium, moderate, and reasonable. But they are not to be doubted on that account alone. Leaving what is considered a reasonable minimum amount of light undefined is not a sign of Byzantine decadence but of classical good sense: the decision is up to the arbiter who will decide on the basis of what seems reasonable to him. More precision on such a matter would be neither desirable nor possible.[1] Nor can we assume that we should necessarily agree with the assessment of a Roman judge: it may be that people living in a modern world where electric light is freely available would set a far higher amount of light (or, on occasion, a lesser one) as the desirable minimum than would a Roman who was used to no such amenities.

The proposed theory amounts to saying that even where there was no servitude a man could prevent his neighbour from building if, but only if, the building would rob him of this reasonably necessary minimum of light. The level cannot be fixed any more precisely. If the same man wanted to prevent his neighbour building at all or to secure for himself more than the bare

---

[1] The English doctrine of ancient lights uses just such vague concepts. Cf. for example, *Colls* v. *Home and Colonial Stores Ltd.* [1904] A.C. 179. Professor Daube points out that it is perhaps not irrelevant to recall the discretion left to the augurs who were charged with interpreting ambiguous signs. The assessment depended on a great number of variable factors which allowed plenty of room for disputes.

minimum of light, he would have to obtain over the neighbour's property a servitude *altius non tollendi* which would be more or less expensive according to the circumstances of the case. It would be, in certain ways at least, a luxury. The neighbour who wanted a right to build even if he should darken some or all of the other man's lights to an intolerable degree would have to obtain a servitude *altius tollendi* over the relevant property and that might again prove expensive to arrange. If neither servitude was present, the 'reasonable amount' of light was what was important.

But how did this work in practice? We saw in the last chapter how some at least of the jurists gave a remedy under the *cautio damni infecti* for excessive blocking, but that remedy was not the only one. The usual remedy would be by *actio negatoria* or by *operis novi nuntiatio*. The aim of this chapter is to illuminate the working of the system. The first step is to look at the formulae of the real actions.

Formulae

Any examination of the formulae of the real actions must start from Lenel. He says that formulae for the following urban servitudes were given in the Edict: *ius altius non tollendi, oneris ferendi, tigni immittendi*, and without doubt the *servitus stillicidii* as well as the closely related *servitus fluminis*.[1] As evidence for the servitude *altius non tollendi* Lenel cites 8. 5. 4. 7 and 8 and 8. 5. 6 pr. and 1, Ulpian 17 *ad edictum*; 8. 5. 5, Paul 21 *ad edictum*; 8. 2. 2, Gaius 7 *ad edictum provinciale*; 8. 2. 32, Julian 7 *digestorum*.[2] He makes no mention of, and does not appear to recognize, the servitude *altius tollendi*. Yet it is referred to in 8. 2. 2, a text which Lenel himself adduces for the servitude *altius non tollendi*. In fact, the servitude *altius tollendi* is given precedence over the negative version in that text. Besides that, it is mentioned in a passage from Paul 21 *ad edictum*, 8. 2. 1 pr, where it is given as a servitude which can exist between two *praedia* even where public land or a public road intervenes. Both these texts have been the subject of controversy and have been declared interpolated but there are no good grounds for rejecting either.[3]

---

[1] *E.P.* 192 ff.   [2] *E.P.* 192 n. 6.   [3] See above, 23 f. and 26 f.

When he comes to draw up the formulae which correspond to the different servitudes Lenel's attitude is at first sight puzzling. Having said that he will give the *confessoria* and the *negatoria* formulae, he puts down as the first of the urban servitude formulae this pair and in this order:

1. S.p. Ao Ao ius esse aedes suas altius tollere invito No No, quanti et rel.
2. S.p. No No ius non esse aedes suas altius tollere invito Ao Ao, quanti et rel.[1]

Judging by what Lenel says just before giving the formulae and by the formulae for the other servitudes, the first should be the *actio confessoria* and the second the *actio negatoria*. That could be conceivable only if Lenel were thinking of some sort of servitude *altius tollendi* when the first would assert Aulus Agerius' right to build higher and the second would deny Numerius Negidius' right to build higher. Arangio-Ruiz thought that Lenel had made this slip.[2] What Lenel actually thought was that in this particular instance the formula for the *negatoria* came before the one for the *confessoria* in the Edict and this he deduced from 8. 5. 4. 7 and 8.[3] There is no reason to believe that Lenel contemplated a servitude *altius tollendi*.

8. 5. 4. 7 and 8 with 8. 5. 6 pr. and 1 originally formed a whole.[4] Lenel is right in holding that 8. 5. 4. 7 concerns the *actio negatoria* of the servitude *altius non tollendi*, 8. 5. 4. 8 the *actio confessoria* of the same servitude. 8. 5. 6 pr. is also a text on the *actio confessoria* of the servitude *altius non tollendi*. The compilers have excised the commentary on the servitude *altius tollendi* which almost certainly preceded that on the servitude *altius non tollendi*. This emerges from 8. 5. 6. 1:

Ulpian (17 ad edictum) sciendum tamen in his servitutibus possessorem esse eum iuris et petitorem. et si forte non habeam aedificatum altius in meo, adversarius meus possessor est: nam cum nihil sit innovatum, ille possidet et aedificantem me prohibere potest et civili actione

[1] *E.P.* 194.
[2] *Rariora* (Rome, 1946), 21 n. 1.
[3] See Grosso, *Studi Albertoni* 1, 466; 5 (1939) *SDHI* 242.
[4] Lenel, *Pal.* 2, 518 and 519.

et interdicto quod vi aut clam: idem et si lapilli iactu impedierit. sed et si patiente eo aedificavero, ego possessor ero effectus.

The text is in a deplorable state.[1] It is about who is to sue and who to defend in building actions, but the crucial words for present purposes are *in his servitutibus*. They refer to more than one servitude. Since the first actions to be set down in the Edict for urban servitudes were to do with building, *in his servitutibus* must refer to more than one building servitude. This has been seen and so the words have been declared to be the work of the compilers who wished to refer to their creation, the *ius altius tollendi*.[2] Such a change is unlikely. For one thing it requires us to envisage the compilers taking so minute an interest in the text as to be able to detect the need to change a small phrase like this. Anyway, *in his servitutibus* is too vague to add anything significant in the Digest, while it would be appropriate in a commentary on the Edict.[3] Moreover, there is no hint of the servitude *altius tollendi* in the detailed texts of 8. 5. 4. 7 and 8 and 8. 5. 6 pr. which deal with the mechanics of the actions. If the compilers were so interested in the servitude *altius tollendi* that they went to the trouble of writing *in his servitutibus*, the least that could be expected of them would be that they tell us how this action worked. None of this is to be found.

A more probable explanation is that *in his servitutibus* is genuine and indicates that Ulpian was writing a commentary on two building servitudes but that the compilers have cut out the references to the servitude *altius tollendi* since it was no longer completely viable in their system. Because the servitude *altius tollendi* is invariably mentioned before the servitude *altius non tollendi* and is so even in the edictal text 8. 2. 2, we are entitled to assume that Ulpian's commentary on the servitude *altius tollendi* has been cut out by the compilers and was originally to be found between 8. 5. 4. 6 and 7. When so much pruning has taken place it might seem rash to assume that 8. 5. 4. 7 and 8 reflect the edictal order, but it will be argued later that Lenel's instinct was correct even here and that a reason can be given for the reversal of the usual order in the commentary.[4]

---

[1] *Ind. Itp.* and Solazzi, *Tutela*, 120 ff. [2] Solazzi, *Tutela*, 120 ff.
[3] See above, 29. [4] See below, 109.

Despite its unsatisfactory nature, 8. 5. 6. 1 provides sufficient material to guide us on an important procedural matter. Ulpian is discussing who is the plaintiff and who the defendant in building actions; the shape of the text can be appreciated better in the light of 8. 5. 8. 3:

Ulpian (17 ad edictum) sed si quaeritur, quis possessoris, quis petitoris partes sustineat, sciendum est possessoris partes sustinere, si quidem tigna immissa sint, eum, qui servitutem sibi deberi ait, si vero non sunt immissa, eum qui negat.

Ulpian appears to state in relation to the servitude *tigni immittendi* that if the beams have been inserted in the wall, the defendant is the person who says he has such a servitude, but if the beams have not yet been inserted, the person denying the servitude will be the defendant, i.e. the person wanting to insert the beam will have to bring an action proving his right to do so. Even if *negat* is awkward, there is little reason to doubt what the text tells us.[1]

There is something wrong with the first sentence of 8. 5. 6. 1 and one would hesitate to say that salvation is to be found merely in deleting *eum*.[2] The *possessor* terminology is odd and has excited comment in the literature. What after all does he possess? In 8. 5. 8. 3 the formulation is more careful, *possessoris partes sustinere*. This is probably closer at least to the classical terminology which may well have been changed, the simplification passing through the stage of *possessor iuris*—hinted at in the first sentence of 8. 5. 6. 1—to be expressed eventually in terms of *possessor tout court*. The second sentence is more informative: if I have not yet built higher my opponent is possessor. Taking it as a simplified version of the terminology of 8. 5. 8. 3, this means that my opponent is the defendant. If I have not yet built up, then I must be the plaintiff in any action, 'for when nothing has been started, he possesses and can prevent me when I build'. From *et civili actione* onwards the text gives rise to severe problems again.

If we can put any trust in the part *et si forte . . . potest* and if we accept that *in his servitutibus* obliges us to look to both the servitude

---

[1] Solazzi, *Tutela*, 124 is suspicious, but cf. E. Levy, *Gesammelte Schriften* 1 (Cologne, Graz, 1963) 413 n. 33.

[2] So Mommsen, *Stereotype Digest*, 151 n. 12.

altius tollendi and the servitude *altius non tollendi*, the procedural position was roughly as follows. If I am about to build or in the process of building my neighbour can prevent (*prohibere*) me. The method of preventing is uncertain. In its present form the allusion to a *civilis actio* in the text is hard to understand; the interdict *quod vi aut clam* is probably to be excluded by a rule that it was not available in respect of work performed by an owner on his own land.[1] Kaser[2] thinks that *lapilli iactus* could be used. This may be right, though one can hardly have much faith in the allusion in the text. There is a notoriously awkward text which seems to say that *operis novi nuntiatio* alone can be used where the work is done *in suo*[3]—that cannot, however, be what is envisaged in 8. 5. 6. 1 because its immediate effect would be to make the person to whom the *nuntiatio* was made *possessor*. The *nuntiator* would then have to be the plaintiff. The method of the *prohibitio* must remain a puzzle.

Since my neighbour has prevented me, he is defendant and I shall have to sue. Where my neighbour makes his *prohibitio*, I have two lines of action depending on the situation. If I wish to build by virtue of a servitude *altius tollendi* which I think I have, then I shall have to bring an *actio confessoria* of that servitude claiming the right to build. If on the other hand, I merely wish to build on the basis that my building will not block my neighbour's lights to more than the tolerable extent and so he is not entitled to prevent my building unless he has a servitude *altius non tollendi*, I shall bring the *actio negatoria* of the servitude *altius non tollendi*, again in effect claiming the right to build.

Where I have completed the building, the boot is on the other foot and my neighbour is the plaintiff. If he wishes to object to my building on the ground that it breaches a servitude *altius non tollendi* which he enjoys over my land, then he will have to bring the *actio confessoria* of the servitude *altius non tollendi* claiming the servitude and so denying my right to have such a building. If he merely wishes to object on the ground that my building blocks his light to more than the tolerated degree and so I cannot have such a structure unless I have a servitude *altius tollendi*, then he must

---

[1] Cf. above 13 f.   [2] *Das altrömische Ius* (Göttingen, 1949), 324 n. 7.
[3] 39. 1. 5. 10, Ulpian 52 *ad edictum. Ind. Itp.*

bring the *actio negatoria* of the servitude *altius tollendi*, again denying my right to have such a building.

We have an instance of someone having to use the *actio negatoria* of the servitude *altius non tollendi* in 8. 5. 4. 7:

Ulpian (17 ad edictum) competit autem de servitute actio domino aedificii neganti servitutem se vicino debere, cuius aedes non in totum liberae sunt, sed ei cum quo agitur servitutem non debent. verbi gratia habeo aedes, quibus sunt vicinae Seianae et Sempronianae, Sempronianis servitutem debeo, adversus dominum Seianarum volo experiri altius me tollere prohibentem: in rem actione experiar: licet enim serviant aedes meae, ei tamen cum quo agitur non serviunt: hoc igitur intendo habere me ius altius tollendi invito eo cum quo ago: quantum enim ad eum pertinet, liberas aedes habeo.

The text is on a relatively minor matter. X owes a servitude *altius non tollendi* to the *aedes Sempronianae*, but not to the *aedes Seianae*. The owner of the *aedes Seianae* prevents him building. X now brings an *actio negatoria* denying that he owes a servitude *altius non tollendi* to the owner of the *aedes Seianae*. The point is that the formula of the *actio negatoria* contains the words *invito No No* and here X can say that he can build when the owner of the *aedes Seianae* is *invitus*, i.e. although X cannot say he is altogether free to build, he is free to build against the objections of the owner of the *aedes Seianae*.[1] The *prohibitio* of the owner of the *aedes Seianae* means that it is up to X to bring an *actio negatoria* of the servitude *altius non tollendi*.

We must now look in a little more detail at what is involved in these actions. It is of fundamental importance to notice that the plaintiff in the *actio negatoria* is not required to prove that the defendant has no servitude. Rather, the defendant is required to prove that he has a servitude.[2]

The procedure may be examined on that assumption. Suppose two houses one owned by A, the other by B and with no servitude between them. A is in the course of building and B thinks that his lights have been blocked excessively. When B asks A to stop, A

[1] Lenel, *E.P.* 194 n. 1.
[2] See for instance M. A. von Bethmann-Hollweg, *Der römische Zivilprozess* 2 (Bonn, 1865), 257 and 611 ff.; Jörs–Kunkel, *Römisches Privatrecht*, 142; Levy, *Gesammelte Schriften* 1, 412 ff.

tells him that he is not blocking B's lights excessively and that he is entitled to build.

B has a choice of courses. He can either use some form of *prohibitio* or he can use *operis novi nuntiatio*.[1] If B uses the former method, A is made the plaintiff and B is the defendant. A will thus have to bring the *actio negatoria* of the servitude *altius non tollendi*. What A is in effect saying in that action is: firstly I am not blocking your lights to more than the normal degree and hence secondly if you want to stop me you must have a servitude *altius non tollendi*. If we adopt what the accepted theory has to say about the defendant's role and incorporate it in our theory, then A has only to prove that his blocking is reasonable. It is then up to B to prove that he has a servitude *altius non tollendi*. Which *ex hypothesi* he cannot do.

Suppose B uses *operis novi nuntiatio*. A will be the defendant[2] and B the plaintiff in an *actio negatoria* of the servitude *altius tollendi*. What B is then in effect saying is: firstly you are blocking my lights to more than the tolerable amount and hence secondly you must have a servitude *altius tollendi* if you want to continue doing so. In order to succeed, B has only to prove that his lights are being blocked excessively. Whereupon A would have to prove that he had a servitude *altius tollendi*. Which *ex hypothesi* he cannot do.

The net result is that under this system, if B uses *prohibitio* A must show that he is not blocking B's lights excessively, while if B uses *operis novi nuntiatio* he must show that A is blocking his lights excessively. Either way, it amounts to deciding if B's lights are being blocked excessively and though theoretically the burden of proof is different the task and the approach of the judge would be much the same. There would be little reason on these grounds for B to choose one method rather than the other. That is a desirable, not to say essential, conclusion to reach, since if A was bound to disprove B's servitude where *prohibitio* was used, that method would be so advantageous to B that it is hard to see why B should

---

[1] For example, 8. 5. 4. 7, Ulpian 17 *ad edictum* and 39. 1. 1. 7, Ulpian 52 *ad edictum*.

[2] 39. 1. 1. 6, Ulpian 52 *ad edictum*.

ever think of using *operis novi nuntiatio*. Yet both methods were in use.

We have perhaps stated the position on burden of proof too starkly, for the classical law admitted a measure of flexibility in these matters[1] and indeed a system where the judge's decision is not open to review by appeal can have no elaborate rules on burden of proof. That is not to say that the classical jurists would be unconcerned about who was the plaintiff and who the defendant. The texts 8. 5. 6. 1 and 8. 5. 8. 3 show that they discussed the problem. Only it was not for burden of proof that it was crucial, but rather for the *cautiones* and the consequences of failure to defend.[2]

When the *actio confessoria* of the servitude *altius tollendi* and the *actio negatoria* of the servitude *altius non tollendi* on the one side, and the *actio confessoria* of the servitude *altius non tollendi* and the *actio negatoria* of the servitude *altius tollendi* on the other are both usually used in similar situations, i.e. before or during building and after the completion of building respectively, it follows that as a rule we cannot expect to be able to tell from the situations in the texts which action is being brought. This melancholy fact means that, although the texts may be examined to see if they cast light on the formulae of these servitudes, the investigation is predestined to failure in most cases. The rest of this section is a commentary on that statement.

The first step is to discard one of the texts which Lenel uses, 8. 5. 9 pr.[3] He was presumably referring to the last part which is concerned with the situation where someone who has a servitude of *iter* over his neighbour's land builds something on it. Paul says that an action can properly be brought against him: *ius tibi non esse aedificare vel aedificatum habere*. The situation is distinguishable from the ones in which we are interested. Lenel also suggests[3] that for *ita aedificatum habere* we should compare 8. 4. 17. Such comparison is legitimate, but the text has nothing to do with the situation in hand.[4] It is of marginal interest at most.

---

[1] See M. Kaser, *Das römische Zivilprozessrecht* (Munich, 1966), 278 with refs.
[2] Levy, *Gesammelte Schriften* 1, 413.
[3] Lenel, *E.P.* 194 n. 2.
[4] On the text above all see Daube, 11 (1960) *IURA* 75–83.

Of the other texts cited by Lenel 8. 5. 4. 7[1] definitely concerns the *actio negatoria* of the servitude *altius non tollendi*. 8. 5. 4. 8 and 8. 5. 6 pr. are also to do with the servitude *altius non tollendi*:

8. 5. 4. 8 Ulpian (17 ad edictum) si cui omnino altius tollere non liceat, adversus eum recte agetur ius ei non esse tollere. haec servitus et ei, qui ulteriores aedes habet, deberi poterit . . .

8. 5. 6 pr. Ulpian (17 ad edictum) et si forte qui medius est, quia servitutem non debebat, altius extulerit aedificia sua, ut iam ego non videar luminibus tuis obstaturus, si aedificavero, frustra intendes ius mihi non esse ita aedificatum habere invito te: sed si intra [tempus statutum] rursus deposuerit aedificium suum vicinus, renascetur tibi vindicatio.

4. 8 is slightly obscure, but what Ulpian seems to be saying is that where the servitude over the neighbour's land is such that he no longer has any right at all to build, any *actio confessoria* can be put in a form which omits the *altius*: *ius ei non esse tollere*. Ulpian may also be contrasting cases where, if no limit was named, the claim would fail for *plus petitio*.

6 pr. is nowadays regarded as substantially sound,[2] though Beseler was doubtless correct to hold *quia servitutem non debebat* interpolated.[3] The insertion is intended simply to make the factual situation clearer. The text deals with the point that the *actio confessoria* of the servitude *altius non tollendi* is not available when the circumstances are such that the dominant owner has no *interesse*.

For the *actio negatoria* of the servitude *altius non tollendi*, Lenel[4] asks us to compare V.F. 53.

Paul (1 manualium) si altius tollendo aget is qui in infinitum tollendi ius non habet, si non expresserit modum, plus petendo causa cadit, quasi intenderit ius sibi esse in infinitum tollere.

Altius tollendo does not fit properly into the structure of the text. This may be the result of *de* falling out. Bethmann-Hollweg proposed inserting it before *altius*.[5] Solazzi[6] on the other hand takes

---

[1] Set out above, 96.   [2] See Grosso, *Servitù*, 267 with refs.
[3] 56 (1936) *ZSS* 90.   [4] *E.P.* 194 n. 1.
[5] See T. Mommsen, *Fragmenta Vaticana* (Bonn, 1861), 20 n. 6.
[6] *Specie*, 70. Cf. *Tutela*, 43 n. 167.

this oddity as a sure sign that *si altius tollendo aget* is a gloss. He seems to feel obliged to argue thus in order to say that the text is about the servitude *altius non tollendi*. No such drastic remedy is required: we can say that a servient owner brings an action about building higher. There are slight inconsistencies of tense but not sufficient to justify rejecting the text.

It may be interpreted as dealing with the servitude *altius non tollendi*. A house is burdened with a servitude that it is not to be raised higher than, say, 60 feet. The dominant owner claims that it is not to be raised above 40 feet and makes a *prohibitio*. The servient owner brings an *actio negatoria* denying his opponent's claim and asserting an unqualified right to raise the house. He will lose for *plus petitio* since he claims too much, his right to build being limited to 60 feet.

There is nothing wrong with such an interpretation but an alternative one can be given if we take the action in the text to be the *actio confessoria* of a servitude *altius tollendi* with an upper limit. This version might commend itself to those who choose to think that *altius tollendo* represents some sort of reference to a servitude *altius tollendi*. The dominant owner has a right to build up to a certain level, say, 40 feet, without objection from his neighbour. (The point of limiting the servitude to 40 feet would be perhaps to leave windows on an upper storey of the servient tenement free from the restriction.) If the dominant owner asserts a right to build and does not qualify this assertion with 'up to 40 feet', he loses the action on account of *plus petitio*, since he looks as if he is claiming what he does not have, viz. the right to build as high as he likes without objection from his neighbour.

There is little to choose between these versions and the question is open.

The next text which Lenel compares for the *actio negatoria* of the servitude *altius non tollendi* is 44. 2. 26. Presumably he means specifically the principium—though he does not say so—but 26. 1 is a help towards understanding it.

Africanus (9 quaestionum) egi tecum ius mihi esse aedes meas usque ad decem pedes altius tollere: post ago ius mihi esse usque ad viginti pedes altius tollere: exceptio rei iudicatae procul dubio obstabit. sed et si rursus ita agam ius mihi esse altius ad alios decem pedes tollere, obstabit exceptio, cum aliter superior pars iure haberi non possit, quam si inferior quoque iure habeatur. 1. item si fundo petito postea insula, quae e regione eius in flumine nata erit, petatur, exceptio obstatura est.

Africanus is talking *de exceptionibus*.[1] The substantial genuineness of the passage does not seem to be doubted. Solazzi, incidentally, queries the figures as unrealistic: with one foot equivalent to 0·295 m. the heights are too small.[2] Presumably Solazzi has mistranslated. Africanus is not talking about a servitude under which the servient owner can build up to the height of 10 or 20 feet, but rather he can build up to 10 or 20 feet higher. The *usque ad decem pedes* and the *usque ad viginti pedes* are to be taken in each case closely with the following *altius*. This translation is perhaps required by the final part *altius ad alios decem pedes tollere . . .*[3]

Like Lenel, Solazzi takes the text as dealing with the *actio negatoria*: the plaintiff is denying that the defendant has the right to stop him building up to 10 or 20 feet higher. The defendant's servitude takes effect from that point onwards, i.e. the plaintiff can build up to 10 or 20 feet higher, but after that he is blocked by the servitude. If Solazzi is correct, A brings an action against B denying that B has a servitude preventing him building his house 10 feet higher. A loses. Later on A brings another action to deny that B has a servitude preventing A building his house 20 feet higher. Africanus says that A's action is undoubtedly blocked by the *exceptio rei iudicatae*. Even if A were to bring an action denying that B could prevent him building 'another 10 feet higher', the *exceptio* would lie in that case also, since A could not have the part from 10 to 20 feet unless the part up to 10 feet higher were had rightfully also and this cannot be so since B has a servitude to prevent A building up to 10 feet higher.

The alternative approach is to see the actions as *actiones confessoriae* of the servitude *altius tollendi*. A claims a servitude over B's land to allow him to build 10 feet higher. He loses the action. Africanus says A certainly cannot later bring an action to claim a

---

[1] Lenel, *Pal.* 1, 34; 51 (1931) *ZSS* 52.   [2] *Specie*, 69.
[3] O. S. S. 4, 544: 'mein Haus zehn Fuss höher zu bauen, es um zwanzig Fuss zu erhöhen; . . . bis auf andere zehn Fuss höher zu bauen . . .'

servitude to build 20 feet higher. Even were he to claim a servitude to build 'another 10 feet higher' the *exceptio* would block his action since he could not build the extra 10 feet unless he had a servitude to build the initial 10 feet and his claim for this failed in the first action. Windscheid chooses this version. Solazzi dismisses it out of hand.[1]

What Africanus goes on to say in 26. 1 might at first sight be thought to constitute evidence in favour of this second view. A claims a piece of land and loses. Later an island emerges in a river in such a place that it will fall into the ownership of the owner of this land (*e regione eius*). Africanus says that the *exceptio* prevents A from claiming the island. The words *item si* which seem to link this case to the immediately preceding servitude case also indicate that they are parallel. It might be argued that, if the similarity is construed as nearly as possible, then we could say that the cases are parallel because just as A cannot claim the right to build an extra 10 feet if he has lost the initial claim for the lesser servitude to which this is but an adjunct, so he cannot claim the island if he has already lost the claim to the land to which the island is merely an adjunct.

Such a view would rest on a misconception of the wording of servitude actions. The plaintiff puts his case not in terms of a servitude itself, but in terms of a right, say, to go across land and to build higher.[2] Hence in both the *actio negatoria* and the *actio confessoria* constructions of the principium A fails to establish a right to build. Africanus is saying that just as A cannot claim the right to build an extra 10 feet if he has lost the initial claim for the right to which this would be but an adjunct, so he cannot claim the island if he has already lost the claim to the land to which the island is merely an adjunct.

It is worth noting that if 44. 2. 26 pr. were taken to refer to the servitude *altius tollendi*, it would be one of the earliest pieces of evidence for that servitude, at least as old as Gaius and perhaps even older.

---

[1] Windscheid-Kipp, *Lehrbuch des Pandektenrechts* 1, § 130 n. 13. See also 1, § 211a n. 10. Solazzi, *Specie*, 69, n. 146.
[2] This rests on considerations explained more fully below, 108.

The other text which Lenel adduces for the *actio negatoria* of the servitude *altius non tollendi* (but again he only 'compares' it)[1] is 39. 1. 15.

Africanus (9 quaestionum) si prius, quam aedificatum esset, ageretur ius vicino non esse aedes altius tollere nec res ab eo defenderetur, partes iudicis non alias futuras fuisse ait, quam ut eum, cum quo ageretur, cavere iuberet non prius se aedificaturum, quam ultro egisset ius sibi esse altius tollere. idemque e contrario, si, cum quis agere vellet ius sibi esse invito adversario altius tollere, eo non defendente similiter, inquit, officio iudicis continebitur, ut cavere adversarium iuberet, nec opus novum se nuntiaturum nec aedificanti vim facturum. eaque ratione hactenus is, qui rem non defenderet, punietur, ut de iure suo probare necesse haberet: id enim esse petitoris partes sustinere.

The dominant view is that except for the part *eaque ratione* to the end the text is largely sound,[2] though Beseler cast vague doubts on it and Lenel drew attention to the odd sequence of tenses *continebitur . . . iuberet*.[3] There is less agreement about the precise setting of the text. Taking it in conjunction with 43. 20. 7 (P.S. 5. 6. 8c) and 39. 2. 45, Lenel thinks[4] it may refer to, and point to the existence of, an interdict *quam servitutem* corresponding to the interdict *quem fundum*. Even Lenel himself was not sure that this interdict existed and others have denied it.[5] The dispute does not affect us.

It is scarcely possible to decide on internal evidence what situations are envisaged. The usual way to take the text is to say that Africanus deals first with the *actio confessoria* of the servitude *altius non tollendi* and then with the *actio negatoria*. Before B builds the house, A brings an *actio confessoria* asserting that he has a servitude to prevent B from building. B declines to give security or to defend the real action. The *iudex* will order B to give security that he will not build without first bringing an *actio negatoria* denying A's servitude. On the other hand if B—who presumably wishes to see the matter settled before he starts building—brings

[1] *E.P.* 194 n. 1.
[2] See *Ind. Itp.* Add, for instance, Boháček, 46 (1939) *BIDR* 152.
[3] Beseler, *Beiträge* 2, 120. Lenel, 51 (1931) *ZSS* 51.
[4] *E.P.* 481 ff.
[5] Most recently Solazzi, 5 (1950) *RIDA* 465. See also P. Bonfante, H. Burckhard, D. C. F. Glück, *Commentario alle pandette* 39. 1 (Milan, 1903), 269 n. 1 at 270.

an *actio negatoria* denying that A has a servitude to prevent him building, then if A does not defend he can be ordered to give security that he will not bring *operis novi nuntiatio* or use *vis* to prevent B from building.

The text can be construed on the assumption that Africanus deals firstly with the *actio negatoria* and secondly with the *actio confessoria* of the servitude *altius tollendi*. In the first part A brings the *actio negatoria* to prevent B from building, i.e. he denies that B has the right to build and block his lights to this degree. B does not give security or defend and he will be ordered to give security that he will not build before bringing an *actio confessoria* to establish his right to build. In the second case, A wishes to build and brings an *actio confessoria* to establish that he has the necessary servitude over B's land. B does not defend. He will be ordered to give security that he will not bring *operis novi nuntiatio* or use *vis* against A if A builds.

Either construction of the text is possible.[1] Against the second version, one could argue that we should have to assume that Africanus deals with the actions in the order *negatoria, confessoria*, which would be odd.[2] If Lenel[3] is right to associate the text with an interdict *quam servitutem* having the rubric *a quo servitus petetur sive ad eum pertinere negabitur, si rem nolit defendere*, Africanus could be expected to discuss the *actio confessoria* first and the *actio negatoria* second. Since the very existence of the interdict is in doubt, its order provides little guidance in fixing the nature of the actions in the text. Once more certainty is not possible.

That disposes of the texts which Lenel uses for the *actio negatoria* of the servitude *altius non tollendi*. For the *actio confessoria* he brings forward[4] 8. 5. 4. 8 (rightly—already discussed above),[5] 39. 1. 15 (just discussed), 8. 5. 6 pr. (again rightly—also discussed above)[6] and 8. 5. 9 pr. (better ignored).[7] He 'compares' 8. 4. 17 (also unhelpful)[7] and 39. 2. 45. The last must now be examined.

[1] Arangio-Ruiz admits as much, though, for reasons which he does not divulge, he prefers to presume that a servitude *altius non tollendi* is in question. *Rariora*, 21 n. 1.

[2] For the order of the actions, see 109 f.

[3] *E.P.* 481. In the *Pal.* 1, 33, the text appears under *quem fundum*.

[4] *E.P.* 194 n. 2.   [5] At 99.   [6] At 99.

[7] See above, 98.

Scaevola (12 quaestionum [titulo—ins. Mommsen] a quo fundus petetur si rem nolit) aedificatum habes: ago tibi ius non esse habere: non defendis. ad me possessio transferenda est, non quidem ut protinus destruatur opus (iniquum enim est demolitionem protinus fieri), sed ut id fiat, nisi intra certum tempus egeris ius tibi esse aedificatum habere.

This text has also been the subject of controversy[1] since it is one of the texts on which Lenel relies for his interdict *quam servitutem*. Interpolations have been alleged but no one has doubted the soundness of the two parts of interest to us, *ago tibi ius non esse habere* (to be taken in conjunction with the preceding *aedificatum habes*) and *egeris ius tibi esse aedificatum habere*. Controversy centres round the words *possessio transferenda est*. In the text as it stands, Scaevola is talking about the situation—different from that in 39. 1. 15 and 43. 20. 7—where the offending structure has been built already. In such a case the person who wishes to have the structure removed is the plaintiff.[2] If he sues and the builder does not defend, *possessio transferenda est*: the roles are reversed and the person objecting will be able to destroy the work unless the builder brings an action to prove his right. As Solazzi points out, the idea of *possessio* is not happy in this context; the difficulty probably stems from a simplification of the classical terminology.[3]

There is no way of deciding between the two interpretations. The traditional interpretation is to say that B, whose land A alleges is subject to a servitude *altius non tollendi*, has built a structure in breach of the servitude. Now A brings the *actio confessoria* asserting his servitude; B does not defend. Possession is to be transferred and the work can be destroyed unless within a given time B brings the *actio negatoria* denying A's servitude and asserting his own right to build.

The alternative construction[4] would be to take the first action as an *actio negatoria* of the servitude *altius tollendi*. B has built in a way which A is not bound to tolerate unless burdened with a servitude. A therefore brings an *actio negatoria* denying B's right

[1] For literature, see the refs. in Solazzi, 5 (1950) *RIDA* 471 ff.
[2] 8. 5. 6. 1. See above, 95 f.
[3] Much the same phenomenon was observed in 8. 5. 6. 1. See above, 94.
[4] Bonfante may have favoured this construction. Bonfante, Burckhard, Glück, *Commentario alle pandette* 39. 1, 269 n. 1 at 271.

to build in this fashion. B does not defend. Scaevola says possession is to be transferred and the offending structure destroyed
unless B brings an *actio confessoria* asserting his servitude right to
build in this manner.

The inscription of the text refers to the interdict *quem fundum*
under which in the nature of things the actions will always be
positive. That does not weigh against the second construction of
the text. Any provisions, whether by interdict or otherwise, to deal
with real actions on servitudes would have to make allowance for
the negative actions also and they would be discussed in the same
place. There is no way to determine just what situation Scaevola
had in mind here.

These then are the texts produced by Lenel. There are others
which may also be relevant. Firstly 43. 25. 1. 4, Ulpian 71 *ad
edictum*, part of which is transmitted also with slight differences in
39. 1. 2, Julian 49 *digestorum*.[1] If Julian bothered to discuss whether
or not the fructuary could use an action on servitudes against the
owner, he was prepared to admit that in some circumstances the
fructuary could have an action on servitudes. It follows that there
is no reason to suspect the opening words of 43. 25. 1. 4 which say
no more than this but make it clear that the text is dealing with a
positive claim to a servitude, an *actio confessoria* in fact. Hence the
words *agere potest ius ei non esse invito se altius aedificare* refer to the
actio confessoria of the servitude *altius non tollendi*.

With this may be taken 7. 1. 16 which, so far as it is evidence for
the form of an action, is to do with the servitude *altius non tollendi*.

Paul (3 ad Sabinum) nisi per quam deterior fructuarii condicio non fiat,
veluti si talem servitutem vicino concesserit ius sibi non esse altius tollere.

In the Digest the text is inserted into a text of Ulpian and is
therefore likely to be substantially genuine. Paul was discussing
usufruct and said[2] that without the fructuary's consent no servitude
could be imposed by the owner on land over which there was a
usufruct, unless it was a servitude which did not detract from the
fructuary's position, for instance a servitude *altius non tollendi*.
This would not affect the fructuary since he could not carry out

---

[1] The texts are set out above, 60.
[2] To be assumed from 7. 1. 15. 7, Ulpian 18 *ad Sabinum*.

such building.[1] This text would suggest the form *ius . . . non esse altius tollere* for the servitude *altius non tollendi*.

Another text which allows, however, of no such firm conclusion is 39. 1. 1. 7:

Ulpian (52 ad edictum) sed si is, cui opus novum nuntiatum est, ante remissionem aedificaverit, deinde coeperit agere ius sibi esse ita aedificatum habere, praetor actionem ei negare debet et interdictum in eum de opere restituendo reddere.

The *nuntiatus* (to call him such) was forbidden to build before he had given a *cautio* or there had been *remissio*. If he did, an interdict would issue for the destruction of the part built after *nuntiatio*.[2] This text says that in such circumstances the praetor should refuse any real action which the *nuntiatus* seeks and should issue the interdict. The reason is that the general right of the *nuntiatus* to build is irrelevant since that right is put in cold storage until he gives the *cautio* or there is *remissio*.[3] Since the *nuntiatio* may have been made either on the basis of a servitude *altius non tollendi* or merely on account of the rights inherent in ownership, we have no way of telling which action the opponent is represented as trying to bring.

39. 2. 13. 10 is inconclusive. It will be examined later.[4]

Gathering up all these texts, we find that 39. 1. 15, 39. 2. 13. 10, 39. 2. 45, 44. 2. 26 pr., and V.F. 53 cannot be assigned with any degree of probability to one servitude rather than the other. The rest can be divided up in this way: 7. 1. 16, 8. 5. 4. 8, and 43. 25. 1. 4 apply to the *actio confessoria* of the servitude *altius non tollendi* and 8. 5. 4. 7 applies to the *actio negatoria* of the same servitude.

The texts which we can assign firmly in this way do not show any marked differences from those about which we must remain uncommitted. This could be accounted for by saying that all of the ambiguous texts are to be referred to the servitude *altius non tollendi* also. However, another suggestion is at least equally plausible: there are no differences between the formulae of the servitude *altius tollendi* and the servitude *altius non tollendi*.

<hr/>

[1] See Nerva's view in 7. 1. 13. 7, Ulpian 18 *ad Sabinum*.
[2] Cf. 39. 1. 8. 4, Paul 48 *ad edictum*; 39. 1. 20. 1, Ulpian 71 *ad edictum*.
[3] 39. 1. 20. 4, Ulpian 71 *ad edictum*.   [4] At 111 ff.

This is the solution which we assumed when discussing G. 4. 3[1] and J. 4. 6. 2[2] and it can be justified in the following way. Although in these actions[3] the plaintiff is in effect either claiming or denying a servitude, the matter is not put in that way. What the plaintiff actually says is either that he has the right to build or that his opponent has not the right to build. What the judge decides is whether the plaintiff can build or the defendant not build. In reaching his decision, the judge will take into account the presence or absence of servitudes, but his judgement is not made in terms of the presence or absence of servitudes: it is a judgement on the legal position as the result of their presence or absence. Where the plaintiff claims the right to build to a height above the normally objectionable, he will succeed only if he can prove a servitude *altius tollendi*. Equally he can claim a right to build within the normal limits if his opponent cannot establish a servitude *altius non tollendi* to stop him. Hence in each case the end result of a successful action is the plaintiff's right to build, but in one the result means that the plaintiff has a servitude, in the other that the defendant has none.

Thus far from being a source of confusion[4] the similarity of the formulae would reflect the nature of the claims, and formulae for both servitudes might be reconstructed on the basis of the evidence which we have for the servitude *altius non tollendi*. The result would be a set of mirror images.

Servitude *altius tollendi*.

1. *actio confessoria* S.p. Ao Ao ius esse aedes suas altius tollere invito No No, quanti et rel.
2. *actio negatoria* S.p. No No ius non esse aedes suas altius tollere invito Ao Ao, quanti et rel.

Servitude *altius non tollendi*

1. *actio confessoria* S.p. No No ius non esse aedes suas altius tollere invito Ao Ao, quanti et rel.
2. *actio negatoria* S.p. Ao Ao ius esse aedes suas altius tollere invito No No, quanti et rel.

---

[1] Above at 30 ff.   [2] Ibid.
[3] The argument applies to all servitudes.
[4] See Arangio-Ruiz, *Rariora*, 21 n. 1.

In particular it should be observed that the words *invito No No* occur in the *actio confessoria* of the servitude *altius tollendi*. These words have been the subject of great controversy in the realm of servitudes generally since it is not altogether clear what their function is, at least in an *actio confessoria*.[1] In his *Palingenesia*[2] Lenel might seem to take the view that they occurred in the *actio negatoria* only, but he was aware that *invito Ao Ao* appeared in the *actio confessoria* and *invito No No* in the *actio negatoria* of the servitude *altius non tollendi*.[3] However, once we see that the *actio confessoria* of the servitude *altius tollendi* and the *actio negatoria* of the servitude *altius non tollendi* are meant to look the same we have no grounds for saying that *invito No No* did not occur in the former. The problems of this tailpiece are not confined to servitudes of light and so happily we can be sure that they do not play any key role in understanding that nexus of servitudes as opposed to servitudes in general.

So far it has been assumed that two sets of formulae existed, one pair for the servitude *altius tollendi* and the other pair for the servitude *altius non tollendi*. However, Lenel observed[4] that the order of the commentary in 8. 5. 4. 7 and 8 suggests that the *actio negatoria* preceded the *actio confessoria* in the actions on the servitude *altius non tollendi*. This acute insight is best explained by the further conclusion that only one set of formulae was found in the Edict and those two formulae were used for the actions on the servitude *altius tollendi* and the actions on the servitude *altius non tollendi*, with the positive formula preceding the negative formula:

1. S.p. Ao Ao ius esse aedes suas altius tollere invito No No, quanti et rel.
2. S.p. No No ius non esse aedes suas altius tollere invito Ao Ao, quanti et rel.

The first formula is the *actio confessoria* of the servitude *altius tollendi* and the *actio negatoria* of the servitude *altius non tollendi*; the second formula covers the *actio negatoria* of the servitude

[1] For lit. see Lenel, *E.P.* 193 n. 9.   [2] *Pal.* 2, 518 n. 2.
[3] Lenel, *E.P.* 194. Cf. for example 8. 5. 6 pr. and 8. 5. 4. 7 respectively, both from Ulpian's commentary on the formulae.
[4] See above, 92.

altius tollendi and the *actio confessoria* of the servitude *altius non tollendi*. The *in his servitutibus* in 8. 5. 6 1 may also point to the two servitudes' being treated together in this way.

Actions

In investigating the actions themselves we have the benefit of a clear account by Grosso.[1] Despite its defects the most useful text is 8. 5. 7:

Paul (21 ad edictum) harum actionum eventus hic est, ut victori officio iudicis aut res praestetur aut cautio. res ipsa haec est, ut iubeat adversarium iudex emendare vitium parietis et idoneum praestare. cautio haec est, ut eum iubeat de reficiendo pariete cavere neque se neque successores suos prohibituros altius tollere sublatumque habere: et si caverit, absolvetur. si vero neque rem praestat neque cautionem, tanti condemnet, quanti actor in litem iuraverit.

Segrè made a very proper defence of the text against a savage attack by Beseler, and there is no need to repeat what he says.[2] The text represents an abridgement of a discussion of the actions concerning the servitude *oneris ferendi* and a building servitude. Segrè thinks that because the action for the servitude *oneris ferendi* must be an *actio confessoria* the building action must also be an *actio confessoria* of the servitude *altius tollendi*. That may be right, but the text is not conclusive evidence for this servitude since, the *actio negatoria* of the servitude *altius non tollendi* also being positive, there would be no great objection to using it as a more or less parallel example.[3]

Paul envisages that the defeated defendant should make *restitutio* and give a *cautio neque se neque successores suos prohibituros altius tollere sublatumque habere*.[4] If the defendant does not do so, he is to be condemned to the sum *quanti actor in litem iuraverit*. If the actions here are *actiones confessoriae*, in return for the damages which the defendant pays over to him, the plaintiff will have to yield to the defendant the right which he was claiming.[5] The result

---

[1] *Servitù*, Chapter 11.

[2] Beseler, 45 (1925) *ZSS* 231; Segrè, 41 (1933) *BIDR* 58 ff. See also Solazzi, *Tutela*, 23 ff. and 43 n. 168.

[3] See Grosso, *Studi Albertoni* 1, 466.

[4] For the *cautio* in the *actio confessoria* of the servitude *altius non tollendi*, see below, 111 ff.   [5] See Grosso, *Servitù*, 274 and 297.

is that the plaintiff's servitude is extinguished, just as the defeated defendant becomes owner of the *res* after *condemnatio* in the ordinary *vindicatio rei*.[1] The *actiones negatoriae* are perhaps more interesting and require more detailed exposition.

Let us once more suppose the case of the two houses, one owned by A the other by B and with no servitude between them. We saw previously[2] how B could object to excessive blocking due to building by A and how he could employ *operis novi nuntiatio* which would mean that B had then to bring an *actio negatoria* of the servitude *altius tollendi* against A. Alternatively he could use *prohibitio* which would entail A bringing an *actio negatoria* of the servitude *altius non tollendi*.

What happens then if B uses the first method and wins his *actio negatoria* of the servitude *altius tollendi* against A? It is not certain whether there was a *clausula arbitraria* in the servitude formulae but the most widely held view is that there was and that Lenel was wrong to reject it.[3] It does not matter, since no one doubts that restitution could be made. So A may choose to make restitution and for that he will have to remove any part of the offending structure which he may have built. He will also have to make restitution of fruits,[4] if any—an artificial concept transferred from the *vindicatio* of a *res*. The fruits in an action such as this would be something like the rents which B has lost as a result of the blocking since *litis contestatio*. Finally A will have to give a *cautio*. In the case of the *actio confessoria* of the servitude *altius tollendi* and the *actio negatoria* of the servitude *altius non tollendi*, the *cautio* given is one promising not to interfere with B's building.[5] However, in the case of the *actio negatoria* of the servitude *altius tollendi* and the *actio confessoria* of the servitude *altius non tollendi* the *cautio* used is apparently the *cautio damni infecti*. Ulpian reports Julian's opinion about this in a neglected portion of 39. 2. 13. 10:

Ulpian (53 *ad edictum*) si quis opus novum nuntiaverit, an nihilo minus damni infecti ei caveri debeat, Iulianus tractat. et magis probat

---

[1] See further below, 112.　　　　　　　　　　　　　　　[2] At 96 ff.
[3] Lenel, *E.P.* 193 and n. 6; Kaser, *Das römische Zivilprozessrecht*, 257 n. 5.
[4] 8. 5. 4. 2, Ulpian 17 *ad edictum*. See Rodger, 88 (1971) *ZSS* 203f.; Grosso, *Servitù*, 296.　　　　　　　　　　[5] See above, 110 and below, 113.

caveri oportere: nam et ei qui egerit ius adversario non esse altius tollere aedificium, caveri debere. item eum, adversus quem interdictum quod vi aut clam competit, cavere debere Iulianus ait, quia non est cautum neque de vitio aedium neque de damno operis.

The text comes from Ulpian's account of those who can demand a *cautio damni infecti*.[1] As an argument for holding that a person who has made *operis novi nuntiatio* should none the less be given a *cautio damni infecti*, Julian recalls that the *cautio* is to be given to one *qui egerit ius adversario non esse altius tollere aedificium*, a description general enough to include the successful plaintiff in either the *actio confessoria* of the servitude *altius non tollendi* or the *actio negatoria* of the servitude *altius tollendi*.[2]

In the vast majority of cases, A would take the course which has just been outlined, but he has an alternative. A can, if he wishes and is able to afford it, suffer a *condemnatio* to the extent of *quanti ea res erit*. In other words, there will be *litis aestimatio* by the plaintiff and a sum of damages fixed accordingly. If A pays this sum, he will be entitled to the right to build which he originally claimed. This follows from the nature of the real action.[3] If this strikes one as strange, then it must be recalled that the damages would often be extremely large, for A would be paying B a sum of money to compensate him for having part of his house rendered virtually unusable, with the resulting inconvenience and fall in value of the property. If A is willing to pay such a sum, he is entitled to the right, but in most cases he will be unable to pay and will therefore take the alternative cheaper way out by *restitutio*.

If we now go back to the situation where B uses *prohibitio* and A has to resort to an *actio negatoria* of a servitude *altius non tollendi*, the same applies *mutatis mutandis*. Here there will be no demolition, though there may have to be a payment for loss and inconvenience caused since *litis contestatio* to A because of not being able to build; for example he may have had to pay a penalty for breach of

---

[1] Lenel, *Pal.* 2, 748; *E.P.* 372 n. 4. Any difficulties in the rest of the text need not concern us.

[2] The nature of the *cautio* in 8. 5. 12, Javolenus 2 *epistularum* is not specified.

[3] The point tends not to be taken explicitly, but see Grosso, *Servitù*, 297. We need not inquire whether the right was actually a servitude or what amounted to the same thing. See further the additional note, Grosso, *Servitù*, 324.

contract with a builder. B will give a *cautio* promising not to interfere.[1] If B prefers not to make *restitutio* but to pay up under *litis aestimatio* he will acquire the equivalent of a servitude *altius non tollendi*. Again the damages are likely to be substantial to compensate A for forgoing his building which might have been, for example, a lucrative block of flats for rent.

To sum up. If B wishes to stop A who is building or about to build in a way which will block B's lights excessively, then B can use *prohibitio* against A who must then bring an *actio negatoria* of the servitude *altius non tollendi*. Alternatively B can use *operis novi nuntiatio* and then bring an *actio negatoria* of the servitude *altius tollendi* against A. Where the offending structure is already built, *operis novi nuntiatio* is not available, but to judge from 8. 5. 6. 1, B will have to bring the *actio negatoria* of the servitude *altius tollendi* in a form of words adapted to suit completed work. The burden of proving the servitude is not rigidly fixed but falls largely on the defendant in all these actions. If the plaintiff wins in any of them the defendant must make appropriate restitution, but if the defendant does not and pays the amount of the *condemnatio* he acquires the right which the plaintiff wished to deny him.

The cases where the plaintiff has a servitude and sues on it cause no special problem and so have not been dealt with in detail, the only important point being to recall that if the defendant pays under the *condemnatio* this will extinguish the plaintiff's servitude.

The Effect of the Passage of Time

The situations dealt with so far have been where the structure was about to be built or was being built or had (just) been built. The last situation prompts consideration of what happens if an offending structure has been put up and the victim consents or fails to take action at the time. There are at least three situations in which he must have been remediless.

Firstly, he has no recourse where the house which blocks his lights was built before his own house. After some time has passed,

---

[1] Cf. 8. 5. 7, Paul 21 *ad edictum*. Perhaps a servitude *altius tollendi*. See above, 110.

finding out which house was built first may present problems, but
we can limit consideration for the moment to the simplest case
where the facts are ascertainable. No one whose land is as yet
without buildings can object to any building by his neighbour. He
has no lights to be blocked. It follows also that even although he
may build subsequently he will not be able to object that his
neighbour's building is blocking his lights: if he voluntarily builds
in the shadow of his neighbour's building he cannot complain.

Secondly, if a man positively led his neighbour to believe that
he would not object to the building and the neighbour built on the
strength of this assertion, it is unthinkable that a successful action
could be brought against the neighbour. Perhaps an *exceptio doli*
would be available, but the matter is not straightforward. If the
very end of 8. 5. 6. 1 is to be believed—and the *et* must mean some
of the genuine Ulpian has been removed to make room for the
strange *mélange* which comes immediately before—when a man
stood by and let his neighbour build, the neighbour would be the
defendant in any action. We may surmise that the neighbour would
have an *exceptio* for his expenses against the man whose acquiescence produced the awkward situation, or else the *iudex* would make
an arrangement.[1]

In each of these cases, problems would arise for subsequent
owners. They might find it hard to prove that the building was
erected with the consent or acquiescence of the person who is now
objecting. Purchasers from a person who failed to object would
not be in a strong position since presumably they were aware of
the situation when they bought the house and the price paid would
take this factor into account. Heirs also could hardly expect to be
in any better position than their predecessors.

Thirdly, if a man fails to take action against his neighbour over a
considerable period of time, he will sooner or later find his legal
position deteriorating. If over a period of years his neighbour has
his building at a height which obstructs light to more than the
normal amount, the neighbour does not usucape a servitude

[1] The details are not, of course, recoverable. Something will depend on
whether the servitude actions were *arbitrariae*. See Kaser, *Das römische Zivilprozessrecht*, 194 ff. with refs.

altius tollendi. The Lex Scribonia forbade *usucapio* of servitudes. (On the other hand, if the building is in breach of a
servitude *altius non tollendi* the neighbour will be free from the
servitude after two years.) Nor will the action *in rem* against the neighbour strictly speaking prescribe: it is *perpetua*. But it has long been
seen[1] that even if such actions do not in theory prescribe, none the
less in practice the passage of time must have had a significant
effect above all from the standpoint of proof. If the neighbour has
had his building at a given height for many years, it will be pre-
sumed that the building is lawful unless the contrary is proved: it
will be assumed, because no one objected before, that there was a
servitude *altius tollendi* or that the offending structure was there
first, or that the owner of the darkened building acquiesced. The
situation would be no different from that with other urban servitudes for which no interdicts were given, for example, where a
man who purchased a house immediately objected to the beam from
his neighbour's house which was in his wall. If this beam had been
there for as long as anyone could remember or for a substantial
length of time, the plaintiff in an *actio negatoria* would find
himself in the position of having to establish that the beam was
there unlawfully. Any other rule would be unworkable. So also
with lights the plaintiff in any action challenging the lawfulness of
the building will have to overcome this inference and finding sufficient evidence will become progressively more difficult as time
goes by. Hence the neighbour's right to keep his building at a
given height will become practically speaking unchallengeable and
he will come to be in much the same position as someone with a
servitude.[2]

As a mere speculation one could suggest that trouble with the
urban servitudes was at the back of the Lex Scribonia, which
abolished *usucapio* of servitudes. Its date is uncertain but scholars
are agreed that it was passed in the late Republic.[3] The urban
servitudes would be well established by then and may have been
giving rise to new problems. Thus it might have been thought that

---

[1] Cf. Lenel, 27 (1906) *ZSS* 80 who refers in turn to the observations of
Mitteis, 26 (1905) *ZSS* 486.
[2] See now Nörr, *Die Entstehung*, §13.
[3] See Watson, *Property*, 22 ff.

two years was too short a time to allow a man to obtain a *ius altius tollendi* and that abolition of the fixed period would allow greater flexibility.

Ulpian may well have been envisaging such problems in 8. 2. 11 pr.[1] Despite certain defects of form the text should be considered genuine in substance and also indicative of a situation where an owner did not have unrestricted freedom to build. The *qui* construction and the future tense are typical of this genre of writing where neat statements have to be set down for the guidance of those without a legal training. A builder who wishes to obstruct his neighbour's lights or do something similarly disadvantageous[2] will know he ought to adhere to the form of the old building. If we ask why the builder should keep to the old dimensions, the answer surely is that by remaining within them, he can be certain that his building is permissible and that the neighbours cannot object: he will be causing no more inconvenience than was caused by the old buildings and if they had to be tolerated by the neighbours so also must the new.

The old buildings may have been tolerated simply because they were within the permitted range. Ulpian would then merely be giving a rule of thumb for guessing what is tolerable. Since the text hints that the old limits cannot be exceeded except at the builder's peril, we may prefer to say that the old dimensions were tolerated simply because they were so long established that no one could in practice prove that they were not for some reason or other lawful. In such a case, the moment these old limits were exceeded an action about the addition would be available unless the builder obtained a servitude. Hence Ulpian is saying that a person who is rebuilding in a city cannot be challenged so long as he keeps within the old dimensions which have become unchallengeable by the passage of time. This demonstrates how mere effluxion of time can come to have almost the effect of a servitude.

C. 3. 34. 1, a constitution of roughly the same date as 8. 2. 11 pr., talks about building *contra veterem formam*. While 8. 2. 11 pr. can be thought of as a genuine piece of Ulpian which is being used by Justinian to refer to the Byzantine legislation about old build-

---

[1] Set out and discussed above, 76 and 78.   [2] A gloss or abbreviation?

ings,[1] the relevant words in the constitution are probably interpolated.

(Imp. Antoninus A. Calpurniae) si quas actiones adversus eum, qui
aedificium contra veterem formam extruxit, ut luminibus tuis officeret,
competere tibi existimas, more solito exercere non prohiberis. is, qui
iudex erit, longi temporis consuetudinem vicem servitutis obtinere
sciet, modo si is qui pulsatur nec vi nec clam nec precario possidet.
[A.D. 211]

Since the text has been causing acute difficulties for centuries it
enjoys the doubtful privilege of being the subject of a vast literature
of diverse views.[2] No attempt will be made to deal with them all.
The opinions can be divided conveniently if roughly into those
based on the assumption that the text is about a servitude *altius
non tollendi* and those based on the assumption that it has something to do with a form of servitude *altius tollendi*.

Adherents to the first doctrine explain that the emperor starts
by telling Calpurnia that she can bring any actions she thinks
appropriate against her neighbour who raised his building beyond
its old limits (*contra veterem formam*). Then the emperor says that
the judge will know that *longi temporis consuetudo* will perform the
function of a servitude, i.e. Calpurnia will have acquired a right
similar to a servitude *altius non tollendi* by the mere passage of
time. Unfortunately the text does not stop there and Caracalla,
having said that *longi temporis consuetudo* will be equivalent to a
servitude, adds that this will be so only if the defendant possesses
nec vi nec clam nec precario. The lapse of time now appears to be
in favour, not of Calpurnia, but of her neighbour; which throws out
the interpretation of the first sentence.

The old way round this difficulty[3] was to say that *is qui pulsatur*
does not mean the defendant but the plaintiff Calpurnia, the
person injured by the building: *id est tu qui pulsaris, id est inquie-
taris aedificatione illius*. Ascoli[4] adopted this approach. Even if just

---

[1] C. 8. 10. 12. 1a and 2.
[2] *Ind. Itp.* For more recent discussions add, for instance, Biondi, *Cat.*,
115 ff.; Solazzi, *Specie*, 109 ff.; Branca, *Studi Cicu* 1, 114 ff.; Kaser, *R.P.R.* 2,
192 n. 24 and 218 n. 30; Nörr, *Die Entstehung*, 55 n. 33 and 56.
[3] It is found as early as the Gloss *ad h.l.*
[4] 38 (1887) *Archivio Giuridico* 223.

conceivable, such a translation of *is qui pulsatur* is artificial especially in a legal text. What is more, the emperor would have to be speaking generally, for only on that assumption can we explain the masculine *is* and the change from the second to the third person.[1] Moreover, only in the most complicated way can one conceive of a servitude *altius non tollendi* being exercised *vi*, *clam*, or *precario*.

That was about the best that could be done in the days before the existence of interpolations had been properly understood. With the advent of interpolationism rather bolder solutions became possible. The leading discussion is probably that of Perozzi[2] who admitted that the last part from *modo si* spoiled the entire rescript; he simply deleted it, as did H. Krüger and Rabel.[3] The deletion now permitted the text to refer to a servitude *altius non tollendi*. According to Perozzi, the text shows that in A.D. 211 there was a law under which one could not change the old form of a building, but this was seen not so much as a 'legal servitude' arising from the law itself, but rather as the consequence of *vetustas*. Another way of putting the same thing would be to say that *vetustas* (which is also what is expressed by *longi temporis consuetudo*) was seen as raising the presumption that a servitude *altius non tollendi* existed. Apart from the deletion of a crucial clause, the main objection to Perozzi's theory is that there is no evidence for this legislation.

Riccobono[4] accepted Perozzi's cancelling of the last part of the text, but went further still and replaced *contra veterem formam* with *ita*. He thought that the words *contra veterem formam* reflected the legislation of Zeno[5] and that, since there is no proof of similar legislation in Caracalla's time, they must be interpolated. Riccobono says that the original rescript was very simple: when Calpurnia complained that her light had been blocked by her

---

[1] Cf. Cohn, 64 (1881) *Archiv für die Civilistische Praxis* 347 ff.

[2] *Scritti giuridici* 2 (Milan, 1948) 252 ff. Referred to with apparent approval by Riccobono, *Scritti di diritto romano* 1, 358 n. 5.

[3] H. Krüger, *Die prätorische Servitut* (Münster, 1911), 67; E. Rabel, *Gesammelte Aufsätze* 4 (Tübingen, 1971), 266.

[4] *Scritti* 1, 358. So also E. Albertario, *Studi di diritto romano* 2 (Milan, 1941), 355, except that he removed the whole of the second sentence. Beseler, *Beiträge* 4, 86 did so also.

[5] Cf. C. 8. 10. 12. 1a and see above, 35.

neighbour and that he had no right to block it, Caracalla told her to assess carefully the title on which she based her complaint. Not only does this ignore certain elements even of that part of the text left standing, but the rescript has been rendered so banal as to be pointless. Such an explanation is gravely deficient.

Solazzi[1] thinks that the constitution is interpolated but he does not attempt to reconstruct the original and his discussion adds little. Biondi[2] thinks that the whole text has been adapted to take account of Justinian's legislation on building limits and the 'legal servitudes' which Biondi attributes to him. However, Biondi does not tie himself down to specific alterations to the text.

All these writers, but especially Riccobono and Albertario, are not so much interpreting as destroying a text which is not defective enough to justify such radical treatment. The less radical approach of Perozzi demands belief in unclassical-sounding legislation for which there is no evidence. Any assumption that the servitude in question is *altius non tollendi* leads to trouble.

The writers who form the other group accept the text as it stands and admit that it must refer to a servitude *altius tollendi*.[3] Their problem must be reconciling that servitude with the usual view of the classical law. The chief exponents are Cohn[4] and Karlowa.[5] Cohn assumes building regulations but the usual objections apply. Karlowa[6] starts off by saying that the rescript mentions the possibility of an *actio negatoria* against someone *qui aedificium contra veterem formam extruxit, ut luminibus tuis officeret.* Also the *forma* which has lasted for a long time should not be altered to the disadvantage of the neighbours 'if a servitude giving the right to do so (viz. a *servitus luminibus officiendi*) has not been acquired by *longi temporis consuetudo*'. Later[7] he says that there was a principle of classical law whereby the form and height of a building which had been hallowed by *vetustas* should not be changed unless the potential builder had a servitude *altius tollendi.*

---

[1] *Specie*, 109.   [2] *Cat.* 115 ff. See above, 82 n. 2.
[3] For instance, F. C. von Savigny, *System des heutigen römischen Rechtes* 4 (Berlin, 1841), 495 n. (h). Cf. also H. Dernburg, *Pandekten* 1 (7th edition, Berlin, 1902), 588, §224 n. 24. He assumes local statutes are involved.
[4] 64 *Archiv für die Civilistische Praxis* 344 ff.
[5] *Rechtsgeschichte* 2, 530 ff.   [6] *Rechtsgeschichte* 2, 530.
[7] *Rechtsgeschichte* 2, 531.

Karlowa adds that with a vacant plot of land beside him or with a house whose form was not yet rendered unalterable by *vetustas*, the builder was free to build as he wished and over such plots a servitude *altius non tollendi* could be acquired.

Some of the details of Karlowa's exposition are a little unclear, but presumably he means that a long-settled form could not be changed without a servitude *altius tollendi* and that this servitude could be acquired, among other ways, by raising a building and keeping it at that raised height for some length of time.

Although this explanation is ingenious, it suffers from certain defects. First, while it banishes the unproved statutes which Cohn and Dernburg invoke, it puts nothing in their place and conjures up out of the air this special principle about old buildings. Secondly and more importantly, Karlowa's own suggestion does not avoid the charge which he rightly laid against the legislation theories: the servitude *altius tollendi* looks as much a part of the general legal order as the servitude *altius non tollendi*. Yet if Karlowa were correct here, the servitude *altius tollendi* would concern old buildings only. For these reasons, Karlowa's explanation must be abandoned.

We may try again. First, a word about the form of the text is in order, for it is not devoid of problems. On the part *si quas — existimas* Solazzi says[1] that Calpurnia would have been disgusted to receive such a reply because she probably wanted to know the name of the action. That particular assertion of Solazzi is wide of the mark, for the form recurs elsewhere in constitutions:[2] the person seeking the advice has not yet tried to bring an action and is checking up first on some matter. Here Caracalla tells Calpurnia that if she thinks she has any actions—and he does not commit himself about whether she has or not—they will not in principle be any the less available owing to the lapse of time. Rather more to the point is the objection that it is hard to see why Caracalla talks about 'actions' rather than 'an action'. There is nothing objectionable about *sciet* to which Albertario[3] takes exception. Slightly more

[1] *Specie*, 109.
[2] See C. 4. 50. 1, Antoninus (A.D. 213); C. 7. 37. 2 pr., Zeno. Cf. C. 5. 11. 1, Alexander (A.D. 231).
[3] *Studi* 2, 355.

disturbing is *pulsatur*.[1] Solazzi does not like *possidet*, but the use of this term, though obviously loose, seems to have been creeping into legal language and it is easy to see how it would come to be transferred to situations which were analogous to acquisition by possession of a *res*.[2] Nörr cites other rather broad uses of the possession concept.[3]

None of these formal objections seems strong enough to entitle one to abandon the entire text as beyond redemption. Besides, Nörr[4] has pointed out how the jurists of this period were particularly concerned with the legal effects of the passage of time. Since the text fits into that scheme of things we must make the most of it. Nörr himself accepts the text though he expressly refrains from making any detailed analysis.

The text can be interpreted as it stands, though this approach is not altogether satisfactory. The house of Calpurnia's neighbour had long since been of a certain form and he then raised it in such a way that he blocked Calpurnia's lights. We can, if we like, choose to say that the words *contra veterem formam* are not really of much

---

[1] Of the two Digest texts where the verb occurs with this meaning 11. 1. 11. 9, Ulpian 22 *ad edictum* is itp. (Lenel, *Pal.* 2, 544 n. 1), while 5. 1. 2. 3, Ulpian 3 *ad edictum* is not exactly happy either and something is wrong with the sentence. *Ind. Itp.* and *Suppl.* Yet to assume with Krüger that *pulsantibus* has been inserted specially seems questionable. *Pulsare* in the required sense is common in late constitutions and is popular with Justinian. Cf. the entry in R. Mayr, *Vocabularium Codicis Iustiniani* (Prague, 1923). Yet it is found also in C. 4. 19. 8 dating from A.D. 289 and the reign of Diocletian. The best evidence for something approaching the required sense as early as C. 3. 34. 1 is perhaps Tertullian, though the verb has the force of accusing rather than suing civilly. *Apologeticum* 9. 6: *quot vultis ex his circumstantibus et in Christianorum sanguinem hiantibus, ex ipsis etiam vobis iustissimis et severissimis in nos praesidibus apud conscientias pulsem, qui natos sibi liberos enecent?* The figurative use suggests that the normal usage must have been fairly well established. *De anima* 40. 4: *sed ea per quam delinquitur convenitur, ut illa a qua delinquitur oneretur etiam in ministerii accusationem. gravior invidia est in praesidem, cum officia pulsantur: plus caeditur qui iubet, quando nec qui obsequitur excusatur.* Lewis and Short cite Statius, *Silvae* 5. 5. 77 and 78 as an example. It may just possibly be one, but it depends on how *invidia* is taken. They presumably construe with *horridus*, but cf. Statius, *Silvae* 5. 3. 69 and 70. Despite *iniusta* I suspect the construction is slightly different.

[2] Cf. 8. 5. 10 pr. which Lenel at one time regarded as genuine if surprising. 27 *ZSS* 80 n. 2. See however *E.P.* 374.

[3] Cf. for instance the edict of Claudian to the Anauni, Bruns, *Fontes*, 253 at 254 and the *epistula* of Severus and Caracalla to the Tyrani, Bruns, *Fontes*, 261 at 262.

[4] *Die Entstehung*, 56.

legal importance; in which case we are merely being told specifically that the neighbour was altering a pre-existing house rather than building something quite new and the result of his alterations was that Calpurnia's lights were now blocked. This interpretation makes the phrase virtually redundant and is on that account unsatisfactory.

Interpreting the text in the same way as 8. 2. 11 pr., we could say that over the years the neighbour had had his house at a height at which it blocked Calpurnia's lights but to which she could not object either because he had built his house before hers was built, or because the passing of time had removed the chance of a successful action against him. The neighbour now built up further and this blocked Calpurnia's lights still further—perhaps in the upper storeys or perhaps he built up a different part of his house and therefore blocked different windows in Calpurnia's house. Calpurnia would then have an action in respect of this new blocking. The major, and probably fatal, objection to this interpretation is that *ut luminibus tuis officeret* indicates that the blocking only begins when the neighbour builds up *contra veterem formam*.

My inclination would be to accept Riccobono's deletion of *contra veterem formam* and perhaps his substitution of *ita*, but nothing more. Nörr[1] seeks to defend the expression by citing Honoré's list of chancellery expressions with the word *forma*,[2] but that list is not to the point since it deals only with expressions like *contra* (or *secundum*) *formam iuris*. Of course there are no conclusive linguistic grounds for suspecting the expression;[3] the objection to it here is one of substance. The qualification *contra veterem formam* would be redundant in classical law: the neighbour lays himself open to an action simply because he builds and blocks Calpurnia's lights. In Justinianic law, that would not be so: by the constitution of Leo people rebuilding were bound not to exceed the old dimensions unless, Zeno added, they had an agreement with their neighbour or had left a space of 12 feet from the other house.[4] The addition of *contra veterem formam* brings the text into line with the Byzantine position. I should therefore hold that *contra veterem*

---

[1] *Die Entstehung*, 56 n. 37.

[2] 28 (1962) *SDHI* 196 ff.

[3] Cf. *T.L.L.* 6 1, 1087 lines 46–50.

[4] C. 8. 10. 12. 1a and 2.

formam, which makes the text awkward for classical law but acceptable for Justinianic law, is interpolated.

Whatever the force of *contra veterem formam*, Calpurnia thinks that she had a claim when the neighbour built up. This would doubtless be an *actio negatoria*. However, some time has gone by since the relevant building was done and Calpurnia now asks the Emperor whether she has lost her claim as a result of the delay. Caracalla replies that long usage has the effect of a servitude only if the builder did not possess *vi, clam*, or *precario*. The form of the text suggests that according to Calpurnia's story the neighbour's building had been *vi, clam*, or *precario* since the Emperor seems to be saying that her delay will not prejudice any claim she may have.

It is plain that the emerging institution of *longi temporis praescriptio* is exercising a strong influence.[1] Nörr refers to this constitution as a text which speaks of acquisition of a servitude by lapse of time.[2] Yet although the provision comes close to allowing the acquisition of a servitude, it stops short and says rather that long usage 'performs the role of a servitude'. Such a distinction, however unimportant in practice, should not be glossed over for it marks a certain stage in the evolution of the thought on this topic.

[1] Cf. Nörr, *Die Entstehung*, 57.   [2] *Die Entstehung*, 55 and n. 33.

4. PROSPECT

ALTHOUGH there is less material available, prospect provides the best evidence that the argument on light is sound. The position for prospect was analogous in classical law: certain valuable views were worthy of protection without a servitude and so a person wishing to block them had to obtain a servitude to permit this; less valuable views would not be so protected and to be sure of keeping one of them an owner had to obtain a servitude to prevent building.

The servitude *prospectui officiendi* is not mentioned in the sources. The pattern of references to the negative servitude of prospect helps in gauging the significance of this. The servitude is found in none of the texts which give lists; there are others which name a number of servitudes in a more incidental fashion, and again prospect occurs in none of them. Its rarity in the passages which have come down to us is due to no mere accident of transmission but reflects fairly the state of the Roman texts: prospect was not regularly to be found in the lists which writers drew up.

D. 8. 2. 3 Ulpian (29 ad Sabinum) est et haec servitus, ne prospectui officiatur.

This short fragment is out of position. Although it comes from the Sabinian Mass it has been transferred to its present place among Edictal texts in order to form part of the introduction to the title. To be more precise, it has been moved here to add a reference to prospect which fails to find a mention in either of the two preceding texts. Other things being equal, the compilers would have chosen texts giving the most complete lists of servitudes and presumably they did not find one with prospect included. Instead of inserting prospect into the body of 8. 2. 2 they brought this text of Ulpian up to fill the gap. This shows that prospect cannot have featured commonly as a separate item in catalogues of servitudes.

A priori grounds long ago led scholars to conclude that prospect emerged at a later stage than the simple servitude of light.[1] A legal system is likely to provide for cases where light is cut off before it provides for those where a view is blocked. Light is a necessary commodity especially in an ancient society, and it would be astonishing if the law did not step into this sphere at a fairly early date. Prospect is different, having more to do with gracious living than with the necessities of life. That is not to say that it is valueless even in purely economic terms, but just to point out that light is fundamentally more important than a pleasant view. Since the pleasant but less important would win legal recognition after the important, it follows that the concept of prospect would develop after that of light.

The date when the idea of prospect emerged cannot be pinpointed. It had certainly found a foothold in the legal system of the late Republic, for a text from Paul's epitome of Alfenus refers to it.[2] The middle of the first century is about the best we can do. The noun *prospectus* occurs in Plautus where a conspirator, checking to make sure that no one is about to overhear, is glad to find a *sterilis prospectus* as far as the street;[3] Cicero tells us about Clodius wanting to have a house on the Palatine with a fine view, *prospectus*.[4] These facts do not help to fix more precisely when the legal concept crystallized. We have to be content with saying it was some time after light was recognized but as early as the time of Alfenus.

This later origin meant that the praetor had no formulae for prospect in his Edict[5] and it is this which really explains why it is frequently omitted from lists, above all from edictal texts like 8. 2. 1 pr. Paul 21 *ad edictum* and 8. 2. 2, Gaius 7 *ad edictum provinciale*. Traces of all this are to be found in the form of G. 4. 3 and J. 4. 6. 2.[6] In the Gaius passage one may note simply that the specific prospect is mentioned after the more general *ius altius*

---

[1] P. F. Girard, *Manuel élémentaire de droit romain* (eighth edition, Paris, 1929), 385 n. 5; Karlowa, *Rechtsgeschichte* 2, 528.

[2] 8. 2. 16, Paul 2 *epitomarum Alfeni digestorum*.

[3] *Miles Gloriosus* 609.   [4] *De domo sua* 44. 116.

[5] Cf. Lenel, *E.P.* 192.

[6] Both set out above, 30.

tollendi. The later prospect comes after the earlier *altius tollere.* In the first part of J. 4. 6. 2, the writer gives the action claiming a usufruct—*usus* does not occur though it is found in G. 4. 3— and then two rustic servitudes, the *ius eundi agendi*[1] and *aquae ductus* separated by *vel.* For urban rights we have four examples, *ius altius tollendi, ius prospiciendi, ius proiciendi,*[2] and *ius immittendi.* Were it not for G. 4. 3, it might be argued that an original list had the three without *ius prospiciendi,* the subsequent addition of which would account for the enclitic *ve* which is out of place when the other links are with *vel.* Since the *ve* is found in G. 4. 3, a more likely explanation is that *vel proiciendi aliquid vel immittendi in vicini aedes* was added later to the basic *altius aedes suas tollendi prospiciendive.*

In the second part the pattern is less clear. The examples of negative actions *in rem* are actions on usufruct, then on the *ius eundi agendi* and *aquae ductus* for rustic servitudes, followed by the *ius altius tollendi,* the *ius prospiciendi,* the *ius proiciendi,* and the *ius immittendi.* These are just the same as in the first half but here the *ius prospiciendi* is fully integrated with the rest and there is nothing to betray its later origin except that it comes after the *ius altius tollendi.* That is no reason to abandon the deductions which we have made. Rather we may agree with those writers[3] who say that there has been revision. They think the revision affects the substance. That is improbable. The second part may be a post-Gaian expansion of Gaius, or else there has been abbreviation and amalgamation to bring the urban rights into the same sentence as the others. One has merely to note the awkward *item praediorum urbanorum invicem quoque* especially in the wake of *contra quoque.* Either the old pattern was not reproduced or it has been destroyed. Finally, it is worth noting that wherever the ideas of light and prospect are mentioned together, light comes before prospect: 8. 2. 15, 8. 2. 16, 39. 1. 5 pr.

What causes a certain amount of difficulty is to know why the writer(s) of G. 4. 3 and J. 4. 6. 2 chose to refer to the *ius pro-*

---

[1] With just one formula in the Edict these are to be regarded as virtually one servitude. Lenel, *E.P.* 192.

[2] Doubtfully edictal. Lenel, *E.P.* 193.

[3] Biondi, *Cat.* 78 ff.; Boháček, 46 (1939) *BIDR* 183 ff.

spectui non officiendi as the *ius prospiciendi*. Although it is hard to be sure while the *Vocabularium* is not available for *prospicere* these may well be the only passages where it is referred to in this way. On the other hand, the cumbersome phrase *ius prospectui non officiendi* does not occur, so far as I can discover. Provided there was no right of specifically looking into a neighbour's house or grounds to be expressed by the phrase *ius prospiciendi*, and there is no trace of any, then no reader of Gaius or the *res cottidianae* could be misled: the *ius prospiciendi* must be the right to have a view and that in turn means *ne prospectui officiatur*. That being so, *ius prospiciendi* can be explained as a convenient phrase, a neat piece of shorthand. This formulation should occasion no more surprise than the convenient term *lumen* or *lumina* for *ne luminibus officiatur* or indeed *prospectus* for *ne prospectui officiatur*.[1] The noun forms, which are all orientated towards the standpoint of the dominant owner, stress the advantage which is to be gained.

G. 4. 3 comes from the realm of actions, not particularly of servitudes.[2] Gaius defines real actions as actions in which we claim a *ius* and we must be careful to understand the scope of the *ius prospiciendi*. When expanded, the expression comes to *ius prospectui non officiendi*, but in saying that the owner claims a right that his view should not be blocked Gaius does not necessarily imply a servitude. In the real action, the decision is in terms of the right of one party that the other should not block his view and that may mean either an *actio confessoria* of a servitude *prospectui non officiendi* or else an *actio negatoria* of a servitude *prospectui officiendi*. The aim of the action in each case is the same, but the factors which will determine the decision are different: in the first case the plaintiff has to establish that he has a servitude, while in the second he merely has to show that a valuable prospect is being blocked unlawfully.

The strange final clause of G. 4. 3 refers to the reverse situation: *ius non esse prospiciendi*. The plaintiff denies that his opponent has

---

[1] For both see 8. 2. 15, Ulpian 29 *ad Sabinum* and 8. 2. 16, Paul 2 *epitomarum Alfeni digestorum*.

[2] See above, 30 ff. and 108.

any right to a view, i.e. he denies that the defendant can stop him building. As we know from the *altius tollendi* situations this will be expressed as a claim for a right to build and block the view: *ius esse prospectui officiendi.* Again two cases are possible: either an *actio confessoria* claiming to block as the result of holding a servitude *prospectui officiendi*, or an *actio negatoria* denying that the defendant has a servitude *prospectui non officiendi* to prevent the plaintiff from blocking his view.

Hence just as we must include a reference to both the servitude *altius tollendi* and the servitude *altius non tollendi* in the phrase *ius . . . altius tollendi*, so we must include both the servitude *prospectui officiendi* and the servitude *prospectui non officiendi* in *ius . . . prospiciendi.*

The same applies to J. 4. 6. 2 which requires no separate treatment.

It might be argued that it is rash to assume the existence of a servitude *prospectui officiendi* not mentioned elsewhere in the sources. Its absence from other texts is not, however, sufficient ground for deciding that it did not exist. It is merely a species of the genus servitudes *altius tollendi.* The qualification *luminibus officiendi* itself is found definitely in the lists only twice, in 8. 2. 2 and 8. 3. 2 pr.—more precisely *officere praetorio*—though it was probably in G. 2. 14 also. This is to be contrasted with nine references to *altius tollendi* (including G. 4. 3 and J. 4. 6. 2). Given the less frequent occurrence of prospect in general, its omission from qualifying *altius tollendi* is not surprising. The jurists would come to recognize gradually that building could cut off not only light but also a view. A further explanation might simply be that *pro spectui officiendi* was less common than *luminibus officiendi* in everyday life.[1]

The best argument for its existence is that the servitude *prospectui officiendi* was necessary. As has been said already, prospect is a refinement, more sophisticated than the mere notion of light. The general rule is often said to be that servitudes are for the benefit of the estate and not for the owner as such. That principle is not infringed by the servitudes of light, for a building

[1] See further below, 139.

without light is unusable. When we come to prospect, we are a
stage further away, for a building can be usable even with no good
view: prospect is for the delight of an owner with time to admire
the view. Even so, it would be foolish to ignore the extent to
which prospect can be said to benefit the land itself. The benefit
lies in the increased value which a good view can bring. It is
plain that a house looking across the bay to Vesuvius will fetch
more than an identical house whose only outlook is on to a squalid
courtyard or narrow street. Even with prospect the estate itself
can be said to benefit.

In choosing to recognize prospect, Roman lawyers showed that
they were prepared to handle an elusive concept. The word
prospectus can be neutral, meaning nothing more than a perspective
or a view whether beautiful or ugly, for example in a military
context.[1] But when *prospectus* is used in a servitude context, it
means more than that: the view is pleasing, beautiful in some
degree. If it is not so, then it cannot be *prospectus* for any
practical legal purposes. In the case of servitudes this can be
fitted into the wider rule that a servitude must secure a benefit
to the dominant tenement, or, to put it another way, the servitude
must be *utilis*. No one would ever think of obtaining a servitude
of prospect unless he thought the view worth protecting and even
if he did have a servitude he would obtain next to nothing in
damages if he sued a neighbour who in breach of the servitude
had obscured a worthless view. For all practical matters beauty
will be what counts.[2]

It is apparent that anyone deciding a case on prospect would be
called on to make a subjective decision: he would have to decide in
effect whether the view was worth protecting. There are after all
views and views. Sometimes without a shadow of doubt the view
would be worth preserving as in the example of looking across
the Bay of Naples. Even in the crudest of monetary terms this
would be worth a considerable amount. One can think of many
other views of this order of magnificence in which the matter
could not admit of dispute. Between these and the outlook on to a

---

[1] Caesar, *Bellum Gallicum* 2. 22.
[2] Beseler takes a slightly different view, I think. 66 (1948) *ZSS* 309.

rubbish dump, which would not merit protection, would be many middling cases where the view, while not especially magnificent, is none the less pleasant and worth something even in terms of cash. One need only think of the modern situation where some people are willing to pay considerably more for a house which looks on to even the dullest of dull fields; when any building takes place which obscures that view they promptly declare— often with a certain amount of justification—that the value of their house has gone down.

There are these different grades of view ranging in grandeur from the superb to the rather inferior. In certain cases in classical law an owner would have a remedy against a neighbour who blocked his prospect even though he had no servitude *ne prospectui officiatur* over the neighbour's land. Protection would not be given to every prospect by this method but only to prospects of a relatively high value. In other words, only if the view was rather good, and hence worth a considerable sum of money, would a remedy be given where there was no servitude. Equally, only in those cases would the person who wished to build have to acquire a servitude *prospectui officiendi*. Where the view was less good, but still one which the owner thought worth protecting, he would be able to secure it by taking out a servitude *ne prospectui officiatur*. Otherwise he would be remediless.

When we think about prospect in terms of beauty, and grandeur, the idea seems curiously un-legal. Yet no one disputes that the Roman jurists eventually adopted it as one of the servitudes. Protecting it outside the area of servitudes would not be qualitatively different: any difference would be one of degree. Moreover, the matter can be reduced to more mundane terms if we remember that it is all just a question of *damnum*, loss. That there is nothing inherently absurd in the notion that classical Roman law granted a remedy for infringement of a prospect unprotected by any servitude can be seen from the decisions on the interdict *ne quid in loco publico*. This was concerned with loss arising from operations carried on in a public place.[1] In 43. 8. 2. 11[2] Ulpian interprets "loss" in this context as including loss of *commodum* and he

---

[1] See above, 49.   [2] Set out above, 39.

can therefore include, among the *damna* covered by the interdict, interference with a view. There is nothing exotic about Ulpian's approach: whether or not prospect is to be dealt with depends merely on how the word *damnum* is construed. A narrow interpretation would exclude it. No agonized weighing-up of principles is involved; Ulpian simply decides what he accounts "loss".

Ulpian's down-to-earth attitude indicates that there is no reason in principle why prospect should not have been protected even without a servitude. There do not seem to be any texts relating to *damnum infectum* which mention it and this may be because the term *damnum* was interpreted more narrowly there. The other place to look is in the title on *operis novi nuntiatio*. Lenel[1] points out that the edict did not contain a catalogue of the circumstances in which this remedy would be available. None the less, in his commentary Ulpian puts the matter partly in terms of loss, *damnum*:

39. 1. 1. 16 Ulpian (52 ad edictum) nuntiatio fit aut iuris nostri conservandi causa aut damni depellendi aut publici iuris tuendi gratia.

This comes from his remarks on *quibus ex causis fiat nuntiatio*[2] and slightly later we find:

39. 1. 1. 19 Ulpian (52 ad edictum) iuris nostri conservandi aut damni depellendi causa opus novum nuntiare potest is ad quem res pertinet.[3]

If *operis novi nuntiatio* was available *damni depellendi causa* and if in other tracts of the law interferences with prospect could be considered as giving rise to *damnum*, there is no *a priori* reason to say that interference with prospect could not have been dealt with by *operis novi nuntiatio* too. There is no text which unmistakably says as much, but looked at against this general background, 39. 1. 5 pr. is of interest. It must be read in conjunction

---

[1] *E.P.* 370 n. 12.   [2] *E.P.* 370 n. 13.
[3] Lenel assigns this also to the part *quibus ex causis fiat nuntiatio*. *E.P.* 370 n. 13 and *Pal.* 2, 744. It is at least arguable that it should belong to the section *quae personae nuntient*. On Lenel's allocation the text adds little or nothing to 1. 16. Also the *autem* in 1. 20 suggests a contrast between the case of the fructuary and some other. The owner in 1. 19 would fit the bill. Lombardi finds great difficulties in both 1. 16 and 1. 19. 32 (1951) *Studi Pavia* 184–94.

with 39. 1. 3. 4, both coming from Ulpian's discussion *quae personae nuntient.*[1]

39. 1. 3. 4 Ulpian (52 ad edictum) si in publico aliquid fiat, omnes cives opus novum nuntiare possunt:

39. 1. 5 pr. Ulpian (52 ad edictum) de pupillo quaesitum est: et Iulianus libro duodecimo digestorum scripsit pupillo non esse operis novi nuntiationis executionem dandam, nisi ad ipsius privatum commodum res pertineat, veluti si luminibus eius officiatur aut prospectui obsit. non aliter autem pupilli rata habebitur nuntiatio quam intercedente tutore auctore.

In 5 pr., Ulpian tells us that Julian held that a pupil could use *operis novi nuntiatio* only if the matter related to his own *privatum commodum*. Hence the pupil cannot bring *operis novi nuntiatio* if it is *publici iuris tuendi gratia*. It is the examples of threats to his private advantage which are of interest for our purposes: they are blocking of lights and prospect.[2] Presumably modern writers take this as relating to the case where the pupil has the requisite servitudes and they are being infringed. This may be so, but there is no mention of servitudes in the text and we have no reason for supposing that a servitude would be necessary. If *operis novi nuntiatio* was used to avoid loss, and if interference with light and prospect could be thought of as loss, then this text can be taken in a straightforward way without having to read into it servitudes which Ulpian does not mention. The use of the word *commodum* may not be without significance in this respect. Ulpian implies that *operis novi nuntiatio* is available to protect the pupil's *commodum*. When *damnum* was held to include loss of *commodum* in the context of the interdict *ne quid in loco publico* prospect was therefore covered. The use of *commodum* here may be a hint that a fairly wide scope was given to *operis novi nuntiatio* also.

But the key text on prospect and arguably on the entire question of building servitudes is Harmenopulos, Hexabiblos 2. 4. 51, a text ignored by many scholars and causing difficulty to those who tackle it. The relevant portion runs:

[1] Lenel, *Pal.* 2, 744 n. 1.
[2] These are well chosen as typical examples of loss which can be incurred from structures on public land, as can be seen from texts like 43. 8. 2. 6, Ulpian 68 *ad edictum*.

τήν ἐπὶ τὰ ὄρη ἄποψιν οὐ δύναταί τις κωλύειν, ὡς εἶπεν ὁ Παπιανὸς ἐν τῷ τρίτῳ βιβλίῳ τῶν κοιαιστιώνων ἐν τῇ τελευταίᾳ τοῦ τίτλου κοιαιστιῶνι. Ἡ δὲ διάταξις Ζήνωνος ἔχει, ὅτι ἐὰν ἑκατὸν πόδας ἀπέχῃ ὁ γείτων, οὐ κολύεται βουλόμενος οἰκοδομεῖν διὰ τὸ ἀφαιρεῖσθαι τὴν ἄποψιν τὴν ἐπὶ θάλασσαν· τοῦτο δέ καὶ ἐπὶ ὄρους ἕλκειν δυνάμεθα, ἐπειδὴ τερπνή τις ἡ θέα τοῦ ὄρους, ὥσπερ τῆς θαλάσσης, καὶ ἀπὸ τῶν ὁμοίων τα ὅμοια τέμνειν δεῖ.

Even though it was known to Cuiacius[1] and had been noticed by Dirksen[2] this text remained more or less neglected until Zachariae von Lingenthal[3] drew attention to it in 1889. It appears to have been extracted by Harmenopulos from a collection of laws relating to building which an architect, Julian of Ascalonia, prepared for Palestine. Not long after Zachariae had published his article Nicole[4] brought out an edition of a work in the nature of a *liber praefecti* or ἐπαρχικὸν βιβλίον which probably dates for the main part from the late ninth century. The manuscript of this work also contains the text in an appendix which gives extracts from the collection of Julian. It is important to note that the readings of the two versions are identical.[5]

For Ferrini Julian's work is pre-Justinianic. He adduces certain reasons. The extract cites Papinian directly and not from the Digest; such citations were forbidden by Justinian. Moreover, the form of the citations is the same as that used in the Beirut schools at the beginning of the fifth century as evidenced by the *Scholia Sinaitica*. The author knows of the constitution of Zeno which is now lost and which dealt with houses having a clear view of the sea,[6] but does not know about, or does not mention since it applied to Constantinople only, the same emperor's later constitution on building heights, etc. Nor does the author mention any of the Justinianic legislation on such matters.[7] Scheltema[8] disagrees with Ferrini and argues that Julian's compilation dates from after the time of Justinian. He deduces this from certain allusions to

[1] *Opera* 4, 87; 7, 398 ff.
[2] *Hinterlassene Schriften* 2 (Leipzig, 1871) 157 ff. and 459.
[3] 10 (1889) *ZSS* 252. Cf. 12 (1891) *ZSS* 75 n. 1.
[4] *Le Livre du préfet* (Geneva, 1893). See G. Ostrogorsky, *Geschichte des Byzantinischen Staates* (3rd edition, Munich, 1963), 180 with refs.
[5] The results of a collation of this manuscript with the other texts are given by Nicole in an appendix. *Le Livre du préfet*, 67 ff.
[6] Cf. C. 8. 10. 12. 4.   [7] *Opere* 1, 446.
[8] *Symbolae van Oven* (Leiden, 1946), 349.

prescription in Harmenopulos 2. 4. 26 which suggest that the ten- and twenty-year rules of Justinian may have been in operation. This is not quite conclusive since Levy thinks there may have been a trend in this direction even before Justinian.[1] Scheltema avoids the objection that no quotation from outside of the Digest would be possible after its publication by saying that Harmenopulos 2. 4. 50 and 51 together form a nearly complete constitution which cannot be dated precisely but must be later than Zeno whom it cites. Scheltema may be right to say that Harmenopulos 2. 4. 50 and 51 form a constitution but it is not clear that in the light of the ban in *Summa* 3 a writer could quote freely from older constitutions not contained in Justinian's Code. If this constitution itself were later than that, would the emperor act in defiance of the rule that all references to the old jurists must be limited to fragments in the Digest? Fortunately we need only bear the controversy in mind but not come to any conclusion on it, for it does not vitally affect Harmenopulos 2. 4. 51.

The text quotes the classical jurist Papinian to the effect that one cannot block a prospect of the mountains. This is awkward for supporters of the orthodox view and efforts to explain the text go back to Cuiacius at least. He remarks that the text tells us something which no other does, namely that a person cannot block his neighbour's view of the mountains. *Quae sententia*, says Cuiacius,[2] *est verissima*, but his explanation is not historically valid, relying as it does on Byzantine restrictions to explain an opinion of Papinian.

Most later explanations follow basically the same pattern although in a slightly more scientific fashion. Costa, however, accepts[3] that the text, as it stands, gives us a genuine opinion of Papinian. He goes no further into a clarification. Scheltema is also against rejecting the evidence of the text, though he would seem to seek an explanation in saying that Papinian's remarks were in a limited context.[4] Dirksen was doubtful about the reliability of Julian's information, on the ground that he tended to introduce non-juristic materials.[5]

---

[1] *Vulgar Law*, 200. Kaser, *R.P.R.* 2, 218.   [2] *Opera* 4, 87.
[3] *Papiniano* 1 (Bologna, 1894), 125 ff.
[4] *Symbolae van Oven*, 360 n. 29.   [5] *Hinterlassene Schriften* 2, 459.

The approach of Zachariae[1] and Krüger[2] is more drastic. They seek to square the text with orthodox doctrine by printing it without the particle οὐ whereupon, conveniently enough, the text says the opposite of what it actually says.

The chances of the οὐ being a scribal error are much reduced by its occurring in both versions of the text. A more important reason for reading the οὐ is that it fits the sense of the passage. We are told that Zeno decreed that a man could build and cut off his neighbour's view of the sea provided that the building was at a distance of at least 100 feet. If it was closer, he could not build. The writer now wishes to apply this ruling also to the case of a view of the mountains: one will not be able to block such a view if the building is within 100 feet, but beyond that range one will be able to block it. Papinian is quoted as saying that no one can block a prospect of the mountains. This is in contrast with the freedom to build which Zeno allows at a distance of 100 feet or more. That contrast is brought out correctly in the text by the particle δέ (translated in the Latin version by *autem*): Ἡ δὲ διάταξις Ζήνωνος ἔχει, κ.τ.λ. If then Zeno's constitution is set against Papinian's decision, the latter as quoted by the writer here could have included οὐ. Cancelling it is unjustifiable, and that line of approach has found little favour during the present century.[3]

The most influential examination of the text is by Riccobono,[4] who declared roundly that the text was not to be corrected but explained. He started out from the basis that in classical law an owner unburdened by a servitude could not be prevented from blocking his neighbour's view. That being the classical position, it followed that the opinion attributed to Papinian in Harmenopulos 2. 4. 51 could not have been his. Hence his decision must have been altered and Riccobono's essay was given over to explaining the circumstances prompting the interpolation of the text which lies at the back of the citation.

[1] 10 *ZSS* 253.
[2] *Collectio librorum iuris anteiustiniani* 3 (Berlin, 1890), 285.
[3] See also H. Monnier, 19 (1895) *NRHD* 685 ff. Brackets round οὐ linger on in the latest edition of Girard's *Textes*. P. F. Girard, F. Senn, *Textes de droit romain* 1 (7th edition, Paris, 1967), 273.
[4] *Scritti* 1, 353.

Riccobono found those circumstances, as was to be expected, in the Byzantine building regulations. Even if Julian of Ascalonia had found the text of Papinian in its genuine form, Riccobono argued, he must have changed it drastically to bring it into line with the regulations of Leo and Zeno, but he would tend to leave in the famous name of Papinian. According to Riccobono this area of the law was in a state of flux and so an old text would have to be changed in this way to adapt it to the new order. Other texts which would have suffered like this are 7. 1. 30, 8. 2. 10, 8. 2. 11, and C. 3. 34. 1. So great is the change in the text under notice that we must renounce any attempt to reconstruct its original content.

Such an approach is unacceptable. What Riccobono fails to grasp is that the opinion of Papinian is being contrasted with the law of Zeno. Papinian says you cannot block a view of the mountains; Zeno says you can block a view of the sea provided you build 100 or more feet away, and this is to be applied by analogy to a view of the mountains. There is no question of Papinian's ruling having been brought into line with the Byzantine law: it is different and what is more the writer of this passage is aware that it is different. For this reason it does not matter whether the text of Papinian is being cited by Julian of Ascalonia himself or by the writer of a constitution, for it is implausible to suggest that anyone would rewrite a classical text in order to produce a piece of law which is neither the original classical law nor the law of the writer's time, but some other sort of law—all for the sake of a passing reference! One may add that if Julian cited the passage himself and altered it he was an amazingly bold architect so to refashion the writings of a great jurist.

The conclusion is that when the architect Julian or the author of the constitution read Papinian's remark it was substantially in the form in which he cited it. That does not of itself allow us to conclude that it was in its classical form. It could have been rewritten in the East, but previously. By the time of the Theodosian Code there were some statutory regulations on building,[1] but we are not well informed on them and cannot determine their scope.

---

[1] Cf. *Lex Romana Burgundionum* 17. 6. See Levy, *Vulgar Law*, 114 ff., esp. 116·

While the possibility of rewriting in the light of this legislation cannot be ruled out entirely, two matters make one sceptical. Firstly, to suppose rewriting in the light of regulations about which we know next to nothing is to court disaster. Secondly, Eastern rewriting is not a theory which is currently in vogue; most modern writers believe that the late Byzantine scholars were concerned above all to preserve what they considered rightly or wrongly to be the classical text. They did not indulge much in interpolation.[1]

The modern approach would be to argue for much earlier interpolation. The latest *Textstufenforschung* doctrine puts great emphasis on early Western revision. It might be contended that the text had been revised in this way. Schulz[2] thinks that Papinian's *quaestiones* underwent extensive post-classical but pre-Justinianic alteration. While Wieacker[3] does not dissent, he reaches his similar conclusion by a different route. Happily we need not enter the dispute about the extent of such changes in general or even in the *quaestiones* in particular. Wieacker is remarkably non-committal about this interesting fragment, and says little more than that it throws no additional light on the history of the text of the *quaestiones*.[4] To accept that the text owes its form to post-classical but pre-Byzantine alteration would open up fresh difficulties. Any plausibility in the case for revision of the texts on the servitude of lights comes from the proved existence of various building regulations from the time of Leo and Zeno onwards, the argument always being that the texts were rewritten to take account of these. This would have to be modified and we should have to assume that some at least of the revision was done in deference to very much earlier, presumably even Western, building regulations of which we have, it will readily be imagined, not the slightest proof.[5] This kind of assumption is fraught with perhaps even greater perils than the one canvassed in connection with Byzantine regulations.

---

[1] See for instance F. Wieacker, *Textstufen klassischer Juristen* (Göttingen, 1960), 172 ff.; M. Kaser, *Römische Rechtsgeschichte* (2nd edition, Göttingen, 1967), 239 ff. [2] *Roman Legal Science*, 234-6.
[3] *Textstufen*, 333-40.
[4] *Textstufen*, 340.
[5] Cf. Levy, *Vulgar Law*, 115.

The correct course is to say that we have a statement of Papinian
and one of the highest importance since it comes from outside the
Digest and has escaped the meddling of Justinian's compilers.
This is one Greek gift which should be accepted gladly.

One further objection may be noted. Krüger[1] says that the
subject-matter of the reference does not square with what we
know of book 3 of Papinian's *quaestiones*, and he suggests that the
book number be changed to 21 where Papinian may have talked
about *operis novi nuntiatio*. Despite the objections of Riccobono[2]
and Wenger[3] that there is no word of *operis novi nuntiatio* in book
21, Krüger's guess is technically feasible. It is nothing more, however, and it is not necessary. Unfortunately we lack guidance from
Lenel on this matter. While none of the subjects covered provides
an ideal setting for the statement, more than one provides a
possible setting, especially since we may have to do with just an
illustration or a passing remark. Arbiters are mentioned in associa-
tion with servitudes[4] and hence the topic could have come up in
relation to *qui arbitrium receperint, ut sententiam dicant* which
Lenel[5] indicates was covered in book 3 of the *quaestiones*. Nor
can a place under the rubric *de satisdando*[5] be ruled out. Matters
relating to servitudes could even find a place under *quibus causis
praeiudicium fieri non oportet*.[6] There are no insuperable palin-
genetic objections to the authenticity of the citation.

To revert to the theme which was adumbrated earlier in this
chapter, it is worth noticing that Papinian does not say that no one
can block a prospect, but rather that no one can block a prospect
of the mountains. This accords well with what was argued above.
Papinian is dealing with an important kind of view: it is not just
a view down the street but a view of the mountains. That type of
view would be worth much to the fortunate owner, the value of
whose property might decrease considerably if it ceased to command
a panorama of the mountains. It would be in just such a situation
that the law intervened to prevent the owner being deprived of his

---

[1] *Collectio* 3, 285.   [2] *Scritti* 1, 353 n. 6.
[3] *Die Quellen des römischen Rechts* (Vienna, 1953), 524 n. 383.
[4] Cf. 8. 2. 11, Ulpian 1 *de officio consulis*, 8. 3. 13. 1–3, Javolenus 10 *ex Cassio*.
[5] Lenel, *Pal.* 1, 819.
[6] Cf. 8. 5. 1, Ulpian 14 *ad edictum*, and Lenel, *E.P.* 141.

prospect, even though he had no servitude to secure it. There would be other situations but this is a good example. An arbiter would have to decide if the prospect was worth protecting and he would consequently have to distinguish between one prospect and another. Admittedly many of the distinctions which Harmenopulos makes, for example views of public paintings, are unmistakably Byzantine, but even though the distinguishing of different kinds of views may have been taken to extremes by Byzantine jurists, that is hardly sufficient reason to stigmatize as Byzantine an awareness that some views are worthier of protection than others. Such an awareness is a matter of common sense and follows easily once a legal system has shown its sophistication by taking the initial step of conceding recognition to the idea of prospect. Working out the servitude of prospect implies evaluating what is a view at all, and if that amount of subjective evaluation is allowed, then there can be no objection in principle to allowing greater protection to views which seem more valuable. The decision may be exceedingly difficult and will turn on the facts in every case, but it is not an impossible task for a legal system which is administered by people of high quality. Whether or not the classical system was well administered, the law was worked out by the jurists in other fields as though it was a system capable of handling subtle concepts. Prospect was one of these and we have no right to deny to the classical jurists the honour which they deserve for their achievement.

Lack of texts prevents us from knowing precisely what views would receive protection without a servitude. Papinian will protect a view of the mountains. Almost certainly, however, no rigid rules were laid down. If the lack of references to a servitude *prospectui officiendi*[1] is any guide, the servitude itself may have been relatively rare. That would suggest that the number of cases in which it was required, and hence the number of cases in which the law protected a prospect without a servitude, was relatively small: the view would have to be particularly excellent. Such a conclusion, however shaky, accords with what one would expect.

[1] Above, 128.

There is no need to stress how powerfully the text of Harmenopulos supports the proposed approach to the law of light in general. Still less need we recall the insuperable obstacles which it puts in the way of the orthodox doctrine. It is better instead to turn and see how the problems of the servitude *stillicidii non recipiendi* are susceptible of cure by similar treatment.

5. WATER

THE problem of the *ius altius tollendi* is not an isolated one. A similar difficulty occurs in the area of stillicide, for the same notion of the essentially unrestricted nature of Roman ownership teaches that a man in an urban estate which is not burdened with a servitude *stillicidii immittendi* can bring an action to exclude any water which his neighbour sends on to his land as a result of altering the natural flow. Just as there are awkward texts which mention a servitude *altius tollendi*, so two texts on stillicide, 8. 2. 2 and J. 2. 3. 1,[1] mention a form of the servitude—repelling or not receiving water—which should not exist either because it apparently gives nothing more than a power already inherent in ownership. To be plausible, any theory seeking to explain the servitude *altius tollendi* should have something to say on this topic also, the problems raised being of a similar nature.[2]

J. 2. 3. 1 supports a common-sense view of the interpretation to be given to the stillicide servitudes. One, *ut stillicidium vel flumen recipiat*, obliges the servient owner to tolerate water from his neighbour's land while the other, *ut . . . non recipiat*, means that the dominant owner is not obliged to tolerate his neighbour's water. Grosso favours holding that this text and 8. 2. 2 give Justinianic rather than classical law, principally because he considers it obvious that a servitude *stillicidii non recipiendi* could not exist in the classical system.[3] More plausibly he says that the

---

[1] The texts are set out above at 23 and 24 respectively.
[2] The theories which seek to explain the servitude *altius tollendi* on the basis of widespread building regulations are in great difficulties here. Only Biondi, *Cat.* 131 ff. has been bold enough to claim that similar legislation on stillicide existed even in Byzantine law, and happily no one has managed to take his theory seriously. See for example Solazzi, *Specie*, 95 and n. 217, and for other theories 94 ff. and 122 ff.; Kaser *R.P.R.* 1, 442 inclines to Solazzi's view. *R.P.R.* 1, 372.
[3] *Studi Albertoni* 1, 487 ff.; *Servitù*, 237 n. 6 at 239.

words *vel non recipiat* are out of place in J. 2. 3. 1. This text,
which probably derives from Ulpian's institutes,[1] gives a list of
servitudes from the point of view of the servient owner. Thus all
are seen as burdens. For this reason the words *vel non recipiat*
come as a surprise since they indicate an advantage rather than a
burden. If the passage stood alone and the problem was unknown
elsewhere there would be a strong case for cutting them out. With
the other evidence this is too simple and even if we supposed that
they are a gloss, we should still have to find an explanation of the
gloss which should not be entirely without point. In 8. 2. 2 Grosso
is forced to explain the presence of *aut non avertendi*, which fits
satisfactorily here, as the result of mechanical attraction. It is
hard to agree.[2] Grosso thinks that the words in J. 2. 3. 1 may have
been inserted by a compiler of Justinian's Institutes to bring it
into line with the glossed 8. 2. 2. Though not impossible, such a
coincidence is improbable.

It is not safe to argue that the servitude *stillicidii non recipiendi* is
interpolated in these two texts just because it does not occur
elsewhere. *Stillicidium* is found in the following texts: G. 2. 14,
G. Ep. 2. 1. 3, D. 8. 2. 2, 8. 4. 16 (i.e. J. 2. 3. 4), 8. 2. 1 pr.,
J. 2. 3. 1.

Whereas enough of the relevant part of G. 2. 14 is left for us to
deduce something from it for the servitude *altius tollendi*, no
weight can be attached to it for stillicide. The text breaks off at
the crucial point.[3] Krüger's reconstruction based on G. Ep. 2. 1. 3
and D. 8. 2. 2 does not include the negative form of stillicide but
this is conjectural and indeed to that extent it departs from the
example of 8. 2. 2. G. 2. 14 must be left out of account.

G. Ep. 2. 1. 3[4] gives no hint of a negative form but is not necessarily to be taken as a trustworthy reflection of Gaius. The writer
was confused on many matters.[5] If the text is intended to refer to
G. 2. 14 liberties have been taken; for example we have enough of
the original to know that stillicide came after, not before, the
building servitudes *altius tollendi* and *altius non tollendi*. It would

---

[1] Ferrini, *Opere* 2, 360.   [2] See Biondi, *Cat.* 132.
[3] The text is set out above, 21.   [4] The text is set out above, 24.
[5] For refs. see above, 24 n. 1.

be rash to conclude that this passage makes it even probable that
Gaius did not refer to a negative servitude of stillicide.

Another text associated with the name of Gaius is 8. 4. 16
which is repeated with certain changes in J. 2. 3. 4. As has been
explained, one may doubt if the text had to do with servitudes in
classical law, but it has to do with them in Justinianic law and for
the sake of argument we may treat it as a servitude text.[1] The
point of the text is that the heir is burdened with the various
servitudes—hence the mention of the servitude that he should
suffer his neighbour's *stillicidia*. There seems to be no good reason
why the author should not have referred to a servitude that the
heir should allow his neighbour to repel or not to receive water,
if that servitude existed. However, the writer is only giving
examples and the omission may not be significant. The same
applies if the text was originally about legacies.

Finally, we have a text of Paul, 8. 2. 1 pr.[2] Again it does not
purport to furnish a complete list and so deductions from omission
are shaky. Furthermore, there are elements showing that the text
is not quite sound. Solazzi[3] points out that the singular *servitutem*
in the second part of the text is odd, as is *prohibendi*. *Supra id
solum* appears to ignore the *via publica*. More important is that
item fluminum et stillicidiorum squares badly with *quia caelum—
debet*. The *flumina* must be envisaged as running along the ground,
but the *quia caelum* clause suggests that the servitudes are prevented because the airspace must be left free above the public
land. This motivation applies to the other servitudes, but not so
well to *flumina*. We are dealing with abbreviation and amalgamation by the compilers who may also be responsible for lumping
together *solum publicum* and *via publica*. The omission of the negative servitude can excite little surprise; nor can any conclusion of
significance for classical law be drawn from it.

Leaving G. 2. 14 out of account because of the gaps in the text,
but counting 8. 4. 16, we have five passages naming several
servitudes and mentioning stillicide. Of these five, G. Ep. 2. 1. 3

---

[1] The text is set out and discussed also above, 25 f.
[2] See above, 26.
[3] *Tutela*, 177. See also Grosso, *Studi Albertoni* I, 464 ff.

is of doubtful worth as evidence for classical law. It is not clear that there is any reason to expect a mention of the negative form in 8. 2. 1 pr. while in 8. 4. 16. where it could occur Gaius is merely giving examples. The other two texts mention it.

The occurrence of the negative form in these two passages is not negligible. However, while the awkward servitude *altius tollendi* occurs in more lists than *altius non tollendi*, the awkward *stillicidii non recipiendi* does not occur more frequently than the servitude *stillicidii recipiendi*. Finally, in support of the view that the references to the negative form are interpolated, it could be pointed out that there appear to be no texts dealing with ordinary cases which require us to assume a servitude *stillicidii non recipiendi*, whereas there are some for the servitude *altius tollendi*.

Instead of opting for the view that references to the servitude *stillicidii non recipiendi* are spurious, I prefer to tackle the problem in the manner proposed for the servitude *altius tollendi*. If we can succeed in applying basically the same solution to both problems, this constitutes a not inconsiderable argument for saying that the solution is correct. The problems are similar and yet none of the other solutions fits both satisfactorily. A solution covering both has this extra element in its favour.

The starting-point is to assume that the Romans thought that a man in town usually had to tolerate a certain amount of water sent from his neighbour's land. If this was so, then there could have been a servitude *stillicidii recipiendi* which meant that the servient owner was obliged to accept more than the normal amount of water up to the amount set by the *modus* of the servitude. The owner who had acquired a servitude *stillicidii non recipiendi* need not tolerate more than the amount of water mentioned in that servitude.

The orthodox view that the servitude *stillicidii non recipiendi* is redundant involves holding that an owner can normally prevent any water whatsoever from being sent on to his land. A qualification of this statement is needed: the orthodox theory presupposes the existence of two different systems of water law at Rome, one for the country and the other for the town. No one disputes that in the country a man had to tolerate his neighbour's sending down a certain amount of water on to his land, and that he could bring the *actio aquae pluviae arcendae* (*a.a.p.a.*) only if his neighbour had done work which caused or threatened to cause damage to his land.[1] Moreover, certain exceptions were made for works done *agri colendi causa* when the owner suffering from the water had no recourse against the man from whose land the water was coming. The power of a country owner to object to water sent on to his land was considerably circumscribed under the regime of the *a.a.p.a.*

On the older view at least, the situation in the towns was utterly different. Perhaps the clearest statement of the contrast is by Burckhard[2] whose account has not, as far as I know, been explicitly rejected. He says:

A generally valid principle, at least in modern law,[3] is this: a person may not construct an *opus in suo* which gives rise to an *immissio in alienum*. So if the owner of the higher land (*superior*) makes an *opus* on his land as a result of which rain-water flows to the lower-lying land, that is an infringement of the ownership of the lower owner which founds the *actio negatoria*. Indeed the mere sending down of the water, irrespective of harm, is enough to establish the action and it is immaterial whether the *opus* is constructed in the town or in the country and whether in consequence the water is sent on to an *ager* or an *aedificium*.

According to Burckhard the *actio negatoria* lies whenever water is sent on to my estate whether that water causes damage or not: the infringement of my ownership is enough to found the action. Slightly further on[4] Burckhard says that where the *a.a.p.a.* system is in operation, roughly speaking in the country, two exceptions are made to the principles which he has set out for the *actio negatoria*. With the first of these we are now concerned:

Firstly the lower owner must tolerate, and has no action against, water sent on to his land with no harmful effect. Since *si aqua pluvia agro nocet* is a precondition of the arbiter's order (*iussus arbitri*) to ward off the water (*aquam arcere*), in the absence of the prerequisite loss the special *a.a.p.a.* is not established, but also the *actio negatoria*, which would otherwise be available, is excluded. The obligation of the lower

---

[1] Cf. 39. 3. 1. 1, Ulpian 53 *ad edictum*.
[2] Burckhard–Glück, *Ausführliche Erläuterung*, Serie der Bücher 49–50 3, 289 ff.
[3] This is a qualification which he seemingly does not take up.
[4] Burckhard–Glück, at 290.

owner to tolerate rain water sent down harmlessly derives generally from the limitation of the *a.a.p.a.*, which specially regulates rain water situations, to the case of harming (*nocere*). In this way the basic principles of the *a.a.p.a.* impose a limitation on his ownership *in patiendo*. But the limitation applies only to the case where the water is sent *ex agro superiori in agrum inferiorem*: the water need not be tolerated when it is sent either *ex agro in aedificium* or *ex aedificio in agrum*. In both cases the lower owner has the *actio negatoria*.

Burckhard is saying that it is only when the harm is caused in circumstances in which the *a.a.p.a.* can be applied that any loss need be shown for purposes even of the *actio negatoria*—the moment you step outside these particular circumstances the *actio negatoria* springs to life again for a mere infringement of the right of ownership even without loss.

It is worth setting out these passages at considerable length because they contain the error which lies at the root of the stillicide problem, namely the idea that the *actio negatoria* lies against the sending of even the least amount of water which causes no harm. Once this is taken for granted, the inevitable conclusion is that the negative form of the stillicide servitude is illogical. It goes without saying that in fact the *actio negatoria* presupposes loss, for without loss there could be no damages.

Just as with lights, so here everyone must usually put up with a certain amount of inconvenience and no action will lie against a neighbour where he causes only this normal amount of harm. If the neighbour wishes to send more than the normal amount of water and so cause more than the normal amount of harm he must take out an appropriate servitude. In the opposite case where a man wishes not to have to tolerate even the normal amount of water he must obtain a servitude *stillicidii non recipiendi*, under which he will be able to bring an action against his neighbour who sends more than the amount (less than the normal) which he may still be allowed to send under the particular terms of the servitude. If the amount of water sent down is so small that it cannot be said to cause any real loss then no action will lie—but this is just an application of the general *de minimis* rule.

I have put down the Burckhard view to show where the source of the difficulties lies. Even though that view does not seem to have been refuted specifically, modern writers have reached the position for which I am arguing. Thus Kaser, who finds the negative stillicide servitude such a problem as to require a solution along the lines laid down by Solazzi,[1] nevertheless says that a man must tolerate a certain amount of water from his neighbour's land.[2] Likewise the standard textbook of Jörs and Kunkel talks of the need to tolerate water within the limits of normal use.[3] The underlying proposition for which I am arguing in this chapter is therefore much less heterodox than the one which I propose for the problem of lights. The aim of the rest of the chapter will be to confirm with modifications the prevailing view but with the implication that it is consistent with a straightforward explanation of the servitude *stillicidii non recipiendi*. Treatment of the topic is made difficult because there are only a few obscure texts on the servitude. Most of the material comes from the area of the *a.a.p.a.* We start off by showing that there was no radical difference between the situation where the *a.a.p.a.* lay and that where the *actio negatoria* was available.

The Spheres of the Actions

At least by Cicero's day the *a.a.p.a.* did not apply to the town.

Cicero, Topica 4.23 ex comparatione autem omnia valent quae sunt huius modi: Quod in re maiore valet valeat in [re] minore, ut si in urbe fines non reguntur, nec aqua in urbe arceatur. item contra: Quod in minore valet, valeat in maiore. licet idem exemplum convertere.

Topica 10. 43 alterum similitudinis genus conlatione sumitur, cum una res uni, par pari comparatur, hoc modo: Quem ad modum, si in urbe de finibus controversia est, quia fines magis agrorum videntur esse quam urbis, finibus regendis adigere arbitrum non possis, sic, si aqua pluvia in urbe nocet, quoniam res tota magis agrorum est, aquae pluviae arcendae adigere arbitrum non possis.

Watson[4] makes certain comments on these texts which he takes in conjunction with 39. 3. 1. 17. The form of the argument suggests, he says, that the limitation of the action to the country was fixed by Cicero's time, but that it is unlikely that any such

[1] *R.P.R.* 1, 442 with n. 30.   [2] *R.P.R.* 1, 407.
[3] *Römisches Privatrecht*, 125.   [4] *Property*, 172 ff.

limitation was laid down in the provision of the Twelve Tables since 'if the rule had been expressly laid down by statute, there could have been no place for the argument'. So far so good: the essence of Cicero's argument is that just as the *actio finium regundorum* is not applied to towns because *fines* are not found there but in fields, so the *a.a.p.a.* is not to be applied to the town since it is all about fields (*res tota magis agrorum est*).[1] On Cicero's argument Watson remarks:

> Whether the argument from the *actio finium regundorum* to the *actio aquae pluviae arcendae* was used by the jurists one cannot really say, but this argument, whether from the greater to the less or by analogy, does not, in itself, seem a particularly convincing one. There is no apparent reason why the two actions in this respect need have the same scope . . . The *formula* of the *actio*, however, would also appear to contain the restriction to land, but whether this wording is the cause or effect of the restriction cannot be determined.

In saying that there seems no apparent reason why the two actions should have the same scope, Watson has missed the point being made by Cicero in 10. 43 and which presumably lies at the back of 4. 23. There is of course no reason why the scope of the actions need be the same, except that both are expressed in words which apply to the country and not to the town. Cicero is saying that if the *actio finium regundorum* cannot apply to the town because *fines* are to do with the fields and the action is expressed in terms of *fines*, then the *a.a.p.a.* ought not to be used in the town either, because it is expressed in terms of fields (*agro . . . nocere*), a country concept too.[2]

Some confirmation of this as a legal argument is provided by a text of Paul, 10. 1. 4. 10:

> Paul (23 ad edictum) hoc iudicium locum habet in confinio praediorum rusticorum: nam in confinio praediorum urbanorum displicuit, neque enim confines hi, sed magis vicini dicuntur et ea communibus parietibus plerumque disterminantur. et ideo et si in agris aedificia iuncta sint, locus huic actioni non erit: et in urbe hortorum latitudo contingere potest, ut etiam finium regundorum agi possit.

---

[1] See further below, 154.
[2] This is sufficient to demolish Schönbauer's claim that *agro* did not occur in the formula. 54 (1934) *ZSS* 253 ff.

Paul tells us that the *actio finium regundorum* is concerned with rustic *praedia* and was excluded from urban *praedia, neque enim confines hi, sed magis vicini dicuntur* and division is usually by common walls. Arangio-Ruiz would delete *neque enim—et ea*, the part which interests us. Beseler objects to the whole text, but apparently Watson finds it sound enough.[1] However, the curious switch to the *confines* and then back to *ea* to which Arangio-Ruiz alludes is odd and does indicate that something is wrong. We would expect the *fines* argument which we find in Cicero, and the compilers may have abridged the text by cutting it out—the *confines–vicini* argument would be suitable as a secondary thrust to back up the primary one on *fines* which would refer to the terms of the action itself. Though not particularly trustworthy, the text is on similar lines to the argument in Cicero.

Watson does not accept that the argument based on *fines* is valid. He thinks that the jurists chose to interpret the word *fines* in a deliberately narrow fashion and suggests a reason for this.[2] Whatever their motives may have been, the jurists did have a certain amount of linguistic backing for their argument. Watson says that *fines* was used of house boundaries as well as land, but even were he correct this does not affect the argument. *Fines* was used of the country as opposed to the town.[3] A clear example occurs in Livy: *nec urbs tantum hoc rege crevit sed etiam ager finesque.*[4] Thus it was perfectly legitimate to argue from the character of the word *fines*, and Cicero is merely applying a similar argument to the *a.a.p.a.* by saying that since its formula has the word *ager*, it too should be limited to use in the country.

Watson[5] says that we cannot tell whether the wording of the action was the cause or the effect of its restriction to use in the country. Cicero at least thought the wording was the cause. This does not rule out the likelihood that at the time when the action was drawn up for an essentially agricultural community it was envisaged as applying to fields, but even if this was the case it

---

[1] Arangio-Ruiz, 32 (1922) *BIDR* 21; Beseler, 45 (1925) *ZSS* 462; 66 (1948) *ZSS* 281 (on *displicere*); Watson, *Property*, 114 n. 3.
[2] *Property*, 114 ff.   [3] *T.L.L.* 6 1, 789, esp. lines 19 ff.
[4] 1. 33. 9. See also Livy 21. 20. 6 for the juxtaposition *agro finibusque.*
[5] *Property*, 173.

can no longer have been plain to Cicero at least. If there was some overriding matter of principle which made the *a.a.p.a.* unsuitable for use in the towns, it is hard to see how the argument on the wording could have come to be used, since it would not have been required. There would have been no doubt on the matter. Therefore Cicero's argument indicates that he saw the exclusion of the *a.a.p.a.* not as something dictated by a major principle of the law, but as a matter of the interpretation of the terms of the formula, a matter perhaps sufficiently doubtful for the example of the *actio finium regundorum* to be cited in support.

At all events, the position of the *actio finium regundorum* and the *a.a.p.a.* must have been similar in this respect. If there was some major principle which excluded the use of the *a.a.p.a.* from towns, then it was a most unfortunate example for Cicero to choose: anyone reading the text would be able to say that the examples were not parallel. Yet in 4. 23 Cicero explicitly states that the argument is reversible: one must be able to argue from the *actio finium regundorum* to the *a.a.p.a.* and vice versa. It follows that the argument must be solely concerned with the wording, since any major principle of law applying to one and not the other would vitiate the argument. We can say then that it was largely the wording of the *a.a.p.a.* which prevented its use in an urban context.

It would be possible to contend that Cicero has made a mistake about the law. This is most unlikely. In his speeches Cicero may sometimes make a mistake in his law or deliberately give it a twist to favour his argument. The *Topica* on the other hand was written by Cicero, a non-lawyer, for Trebatius, a jurist. In such circumstances he would take the greatest care to ensure that his legal examples were sound, and he would also be likely to choose straightforward illustrations. We should hesitate a long time before saying that Cicero is mistaken about the law here.

To sum up so far, we may deduce from these passages in Cicero that he thought that the *a.a.p.a.* did not apply to the town, but the reason for this was that the wording of the action suited only the country. These conclusions are borne out when we consider the reports which the Digest has preserved on this matter. Indeed the Digest texts are far from suggesting any basic differences between the *a.a.p.a.* in the country and the *actio negatoria.* The key text is 39. 3. 1. 17.

Ulpian (53 ad edictum) item sciendum est hanc actionem non alias locum habere, quam si aqua pluvia agro noceat: ceterum si aedificio vel oppido noceat, cessat actio ista, agi autem ita poterit ius non esse stillicidia flumina immittere. et ideo Labeo et Cascellius aiunt aquae quidem pluviae arcendae actionem specialem esse, de fluminibus et stillicidiis generalem et ubique agi ea licere. itaque aqua, quae agro nocet, per aquae pluviae arcendae actionem coercebitur.

Ulpian says that the *a.a.p.a.* does not apply except when there is damage to a field; if there is damage to a building or town this action does not lie, but an action can be brought alleging *ius non esse stillicidia flumina immittere.* Labeo and Cascellius say the *a.a.p.a.* is special whereas the action on *flumina* and *stillicidia* is general and can be used in all cases. So water which damages a field will be checked by the *a.a.p.a.*

In a study of *iste* Beseler held that much of this text is spurious.[1] He was followed by Albertario, followed in his turn by Pringsheim. Beseler wished to delete *vel oppido* (which does indeed look like a gloss), *ista–immittere,* and *aquae quidem–coercebitur.* To the first part he objects 'As if the house-owner could ward off all rain water as *stillicidium* or *flumen!*' while the bit after *aiunt* he regards as empty Byzantine systematizing. He further takes exception to *ubique* meaning 'in all cases'. Biondi also considers the text interpolated to a lesser, undefined extent but he cites Lenel in support and yet Lenel does not seem to be suspicious about it.[2]

Beseler's radical attack on this text is hard to accept and has by no means gone unchallenged. Levy[3] pointed out that it was unlikely that such a specific reference to the wording of an action would derive from a Byzantine source, and Beseler's reply that the

[1] For the literature on the text see *Ind. Itp.* and add Beseler, 45 (1925) *ZSS* 478; Biondi, *Cat.* 167; Grosso, 3 (1937) *SDHI* 290; Sargenti, *Studi de Francisci* 3 (Milan, 1956), 352 n. 3; G. Branca, *Danno temuto e danno da cose inanimate* (Padua, 1937), 392 n. 2; Watson, *Property*, 172 ff. and 196.
[2] See *E.P.* 194 n. 7. Biondi cites *E.P.* 377 but the passage is not mentioned there.
[3] *Konkurrenz der Aktionen* 1 (Berlin, 1918), 276 n. 5.

pre-Justinianic Byzantines took a lively interest in classical formulary procedure does not really answer Levy fully. Bonfante[1] also thought Beseler's attack misconceived and said that the text does not mean that the owner can ward off all rain water as *stillicidium* or *flumen*, but rather that the requirement of an *opus* is to be understood—we shall come back to this later.[2] Grosso, Sargenti, Branca, and Watson (tacitly) all take the passage as substantially genuine.

This is correct. The reference to Labeo and Cascellius must be genuine—note the typical anti-chronological order.[3] The rest of that sentence is grammatically unexceptionable. Of course, the passage has probably been abridged, because the last sentence does not fit with the one before it—if the action on *stillicidia* and *flumina* is general, it does not follow (*itaque*) that we must use the *a.a.p.a.* in the case of harm to a field.

Yet if the passage is largely genuine, on the traditional view of urban waters Ulpian must be talking very loosely indeed. According to that view, outside the range of the *a.a.p.a.* an owner had the right to ward off any water which was sent on to his land, even though it did no damage. In this Burckhard view the *actio negatoria* is completely different from the *a.a.p.a.* which requires proof of damage, actual or threatened. Yet Ulpian speaks in sweeping terms which lead us to believe that the actions are similar, the *a.a.p.a.* being limited to damage to fields while the stillicide action is, if we take Labeo and Cascellius at face value, available everywhere, i.e. not only in cases of damage to fields. If it was not in practice used in the case of fields then that was because a special action existed. The passage gives the impression that the *a.a.p.a.* was an old exception. The *actio negatoria* would have been capable of dealing with the situation in the case of fields, but there was already in existence the very ancient *a.a.p.a.*—certainly as early as the Twelve Tables—and this maintained its somewhat anomalous position in the face of the later but more flexible *actio negatoria*. Ulpian may have been aware of an essential difference

---

[1] *Corso* 2 1, 426 n. 1.   [2] At 160 ff.
[3] Cf. the passages in Lenel, *Pal.* 1, 107 ff. On the significance of this see A. M. Honoré, *Gaius* (Oxford, 1962), xvi ff.

between the actions, but if so, he manages successfully to convey the opposite impression.

We are told of decisions on the scope of the action which must turn on the wording of the *a.a.p.a.* but which give no grounds for believing that the actions were radically different.

39. 3. 1. 18 Ulpian (53 ad edictum) nec illud quaeramus, unde oriatur: nam et si publico oriens vel ex loco sacro per fundum vicini descendat isque opere facto in meum fundum eam avertat, aquae pluviae arcendae teneri eum Labeo ait.   19. Cassius quoque scribit, si aqua ex aedificio urbano noceat vel agro vel aedificio rustico, agendum de fluminibus et stillicidiis.   20. apud Labeonem autem invenio relatum, si ex agro meo aqua fluens noceat loco qui est intra continentia [hoc est aedificio], non posse me aquae pluviae arcendae conveniri: quod si ex continentibus profluens in meum agrum defluat eique noceat, aquae pluviae arcendae esse actionem.

The words in square brackets are a gloss.[1] In 1. 19 we have Cassius' opinion that if a field or rural building were damaged by water from an urban building the action *de fluminibus et stillicidiis* should be brought. In 1. 20, while Labeo would not admit the *a.a.p.a.* where water from a field did damage to a place in the outskirts of a town, he would allow it where water from the suburbs did damage to a field. The contrast with the decision of Cassius in the previous section makes it plain that the *opus*, which is not mentioned, is also supposed to be in the suburbs.

This ruling of Labeo casts substantial doubt on the accuracy of Lenel's reconstruction of the formula for the *a.a.p.a.*[2] Lenel composes the relevant part: *S.p. opus factum esse in agro Capenate, unde aqua pluvia agro Ai Ai nocet. . . .* Now if Lenel is right, Labeo is juggling with the meaning of *ager* in a remarkable way. Always supposing Lenel is correct, Labeo first says that the object of the damage cannot be urban because the wording of the formula has *agro Ai Ai nocet*, but then in allowing the action when water from the suburbs did damage to a field, he ignores the provision that the *opus* be *in agro Capenate*. Such a conflicting interpreta-

[1] Lenel, *Pal.* 2, 754 n. 1.
[2] Doubts have been expressed several times especially by Karlowa, Schönbauer, and recently Kaser, 83 (1966) *ZSS* 39 ff. with refs. Watson, *Property*, 155 ff. treats it as settled.

tion of the same word *ager* in the same formula would be rather surprising. The best way out of the difficulty is to say that the words *in agro Capenate* were not in the formula.

Lenel claims to find support for his reconstruction of the part *S.p.–nocet* in 39. 3. 1 and 39. 3. 3 pr.–2 along with certain other passages which he cites.[1] Despite what he says there is nothing in any of them which justifies *in agro Capenate*. In the only text among them which uses *in agro*, 39. 3. 14. 1, Paul 49 *ad edictum* the words have nothing to do with this matter. The text is about the problems which arise because liability is for an *opus manu factum*, and Paul says that no *a.a.p.a.* lies where the damage is the result of subsidence due to a *vitium loci*. He then adds that perhaps the same is to be said if a man-made object in the field subsides and damage results. In other words in the case of subsidence there may be no liability even though it involves an *opus manu factum*. The only passage which might just possibly be thought to give some help to Lenel is *Topica* 10.43 where Cicero says *res tota magis agrorum est* but Lenel rightly takes this as referring to the *agro Ai Ai* part only.[2] Lenel himself may at one time have had doubts: we find in the *Palingenesia* a footnote with the variant form *s.p. opus factum esse in fundo illo, unde agro Ai Ai aqua pluvia noceret.*[3]

Kaser has recently[4] rejected Lenel's formulation and has proposed something like:

S.p. Nm Nm aquam pluviam, quae ex opere in agro Capenate facto agro Ai Ai nocet, arcere oportere, neque ea res arbitrio tuo restituetur, quanti ea res erit . . .

Kaser claims that his reconstruction fits the structure of the commentary. Whatever may be said about the rest of it, the first part does not.

In 39. 3. 1 pr. there is what at first sight looks like a commentary on the element *aqua pluvia* in the formula—hence, I suppose, Kaser puts these words at the start. However, 1 pr. is just a general introduction to the commentary,[5] which does not start properly

---

[1] *E.P.* 375 n. 5.					[2] *E.P.* 375 n. 5.
[3] *Pal.* 2, 753 n. 1 . His doubts never penetrated to his *E.P.*
[4] 83 (1966) *ZSS* 39 ff.					[5] Cf. 39. 1. 1 pr., Ulpian 52 *ad edictum*.

until 1. 1 when Ulpian explains about *opus*. His commentary on various aspects of *opus* continues down to 1. 15 and includes among other things the exemption of an *opus* for agricultural purposes (1. 3–1. 9) and the non-actionability of natural damage (1. 14). A résumé is given in 1. 15.

1. 16 is curious and by no means fits in with 1.15 even though it is in indirect speech. Something has been omitted between the texts and since 1. 16 is obviously an elucidation of some statement containing a phrase like *aqua quae imbre crescit,*[1] it presumably represents all that the compilers have retained here of Ulpian's commentary on the term *aqua pluvia.*[2]

With 1. 17 we hasten on to a different matter, namely the requirement that the damage be to a field, *agro*. Merely as an adjunct to that, in 1. 18 Ulpian brings up the question of the origin of the water, which he treats as unimportant since all that matters is that the neighbour diverts it with an *opus*. 1. 19 and 1. 20 contain the remarks on an *opus* in the town, while in 1. 21 Ulpian proceeds to look at the scope of *nocere*.

On the strength of such an analysis we obtain the order *opus–aqua pluvia–agro–nocere.*[3] Lenel's formula would require *opus–in agro Capenate–aqua pluvia–agro–nocere*. For that we should need something on *in agro Capenate* between 1. 15 and 1. 16, but any remarks on the situation of the *opus* come in 1. 19 and 1. 20. Kaser's order would be: *Nm Nm–aqua pluvia–opus–in agro Capenate–agro–nocere*. Here three elements are astray: the defendant Numerius Negidius does not appear in this section of the commentary;[4] *aqua pluvia* precedes, instead of coming after, *opus* and *in agro Capenate* runs into the same problems as in Lenel's version. A version similar to Lenel's but which would conform more nearly to the shape of the commentary would have to begin:

S.p. opere facto[5] aquam pluviam agro Ai Ai nocere . . .

[1] Cf. 39. 3. 1 pr., Ulpian 53 *ad edictum* and Cicero, *Topica* 9. 39.
[2] See below, 165 n. 3.
[3] Schönbauer's doubts extend much too far.
[4] Kaser himself does not envisage discussion of the defendant till the same part as Lenel, *E.P.* 377 n. 3, but Lenel's version fits the commentary more snugly.
[5] Cf. 39. 3. 1. 1; 1. 10; 1. 13; 1. 15; 1. 21.

If Kaser's criticisms of Lenel's version were accepted, then an equivalent reshaping of his own production could doubtless be made.

I cannot see that much is lost. If the phrase *in agro Capenate* occurred it would be the peg on which to hang a discussion of the *opus* on public land, *in publico*. But it does not occur in such contexts. Rather, in relation to the defendant in the action, Ulpian argues that juristic interpretation has established that only a person who does work *in suo* should be liable and so one who does work *in publico* cannot be liable.[1] In 39. 3. 4 pr. Ulpian defines the defendant in terms of the owner of the *opus*, and in 39. 3. 18, Javolenus 10 *ex Cassio* the exclusion of work *in publico* is explained as a consequence of lack of ownership. Both the silence about the ownership of the land and the slightly indirect way of determining the *in publico* cases are explained most easily on the hypothesis that the words *in agro Capenate* are figments of modern scholarship.

Moreover, reverting to our point of departure, if there were such a phrase, we should expect the action to be limited to an *opus* constructed in the country. With the formula silent on the question, Cassius might argue that the ethos of the action was rural and that it should be confined to the country by implying that the *opus* must be *in agro* also, while Labeo might feel that, there being no explicit statement in the formula, the action should not be restricted in this way. This amounts to a difference of opinion between the Proculian Labeo and the slightly later Sabinian Cassius, but we cannot tell whether or not this was in any sense a 'school dispute'—at all events the dispute would be of little practical importance.

This is a suitable point for a digression on the sphere of application of the servitude of *stillicidia* and *flumina*. As a problem it touches at several points on another about a so-called servitude *aquae immittendae*. The very existence of this servitude has been doubted by Solazzi[2] and denied by Sargenti,[3] but the particular

---

[1] 39. 3. 3. 3, Ulpian 53 *ad edictum*. Lenel, *Pal.* 2, 755 n. 1; *E.P.* 377 n. 3. The reconstruction of the formula, which is advanced on the basis of this text by Peters, 35 (1969) *SDHI* 166 ff., should not have been possible after Lenel's work.

[2] *Specie*, 117. [3] *Studi de Francisci* 3, 352.

thesis is quite untenable and not worth refuting in detail. It is sufficient to notice the explicit references in 39. 3. 2. 10 and 43. 8. 2. 28. 8. 3. 29 also deals with such a case, even though the verb used is *educere*.[1]

Grosso speaks of a servitude of uncertain content of which the details were gradually worked out by the jurists.[2] His argument is hard to understand, but he hints at what may have been the facts of the situation. Unfortunately evidence is in short supply. What existed, probably in an urban context initially, was a servitude right to send water on to your neighbour's land in excess of the usual amount, but this servitude would have a different content and form in different situations. In an urban setting, what is wanted is the right to drop water from the eaves of your house on to your neighbour's land or house. You might also want to drain rain water in gutters on to his land. In rural conditions, these would not be the usual demands. We should think rather of the right to drain streams of water from one field down to a neighbour's field by means of irrigation channels. Occasionally there would be a degree of overlapping when practices more common in the country would be desired by a particular owner in the town and vice versa, but these would be exceptional cases. Though the content of the servitude would be different in this way in different areas, it would be in essence the same servitude of sending water on to a neighbour's land.

One may envisage a historical development along these lines. Already in the time of the Twelve Tables the *a.a.p.a.* provided a remedy where water did damage to fields. This would be the most important case at that period and would remain so for some time. However, with the development of the town, the urban servitudes emerged and among them was the servitude of *stillicidia* and *flumina* to help regulate water in an urban context, the *a.a.p.a.* with its *agro nocere* not being appropriate there. The stillicide servitude began as one of those connected with towns, and this explains why it features in lists of urban servitudes in legal writings and is associated with them even as early as Cicero,[3]

---

[1] So Watson, *Property*, 195.   [2] 3 *SDHI* 290.
[3] For example, *de oratore* 1. 38. 173.

while Varro also connected a clause on *stillicidia fluminaque* with contracts relating to urban land.[1] Though it started in the towns, people came to think that the water servitude might also be applicable in the country, and this opinion was successful probably about the beginning of the first century B.C., for two texts dealing with the matter refer to that period.

> 39. 3. 2. 10 Paul (49 ad edictum) illud etiam verum puto, quod Ofilius scribit, si fundus tuus vicino serviat et propterea aquam recipiat, cessare aquae pluviae arcendae actionem [sic tamen, si non ultra modum noceat]. cui consequens est, quod Labeo putat si quis vicino cesserit ius ei esse aquam immittere, aquae pluviae arcendae eum agere non posse.

The part in brackets is almost certainly interpolated.[2] For the moment the question of the authenticity of the rest, which is challenged by Solazzi alone, can be left on one side. Ofilius thought that if there was a servitude under which one piece of land took another's water, the *a.a.p.a.* was excluded. The *puto* of Paul suggests that surprisingly enough even some three centuries later there was doubt about it. It is not improbable that Ofilius' view was preserved just because he was one of the first to recognize that the *a.a.p.a.* could be excluded in this way, and this would mean that the water servitude affecting the question had developed later on nearer his time. Admittedly, the text does not give the servitude a name, but in 39. 3. 1. 17 we have already noted the opinion of a jurist of roughly the same time, Cascellius, who says that the action *de fluminibus et stillicidiis* is general and can be used *ubique*.[3] It may just be a coincidence that two jurists of this early vintage are quoted in this connection, but it suggests that the applicability of the water servitude in the country was being worked out about then, and what happened was that an extension was made from the town to the country.

If, then, the texts use different terms to describe water servitudes, these terms may just serve to indicate the content of the servitude in that instance. So all three texts noted above for the (so-called)

---

[1] Varro, *de lingua latina* 5. 27.
[2] Cf. *Ind. Itp.* and Watson, *Property*, 173 ff. with refs.
[3] See above, 151 f.

servitude *aquae immittendae* deal with rural situations, and probably in each the object is to ensure drainage for the dominant land. The typical texts on *stillicidia* are from an urban context where the water servitude would most often assume this form. If the servitude was originally *stillicidia et flumina* in the towns and was taken over in the country, this explains why that name persists in the lists and why it could also be used by Cascellius even with reference to the country. On the other hand, it would be only natural if other more appropriate ways of referring to the servitude of water in the country were evolved also, and this explains the references to the servitude of receiving water to which Solazzi objected. It was not indeed another servitude, simply one form of the same servitude of water.

Should this theory be correct, the point of the dispute about the availability of the *a.a.p.a.* or the *actio negatoria* in the borderline cases can in no sense be a reflection of an idea that the servitude of *stillicidia* and *flumina* was an urban servitude of which the *actio negatoria* should not be available in the country.[1] Rather the argument is the other way round: the *a.a.p.a.* is by its very wording a rural action and should not be applied to urban cases. The *actio negatoria* fills the gaps where it does not apply for this reason. But again it is noteworthy that there is no hint that the consequences of giving one action rather than the other were crucially important. Far from it: we gain the impression that the actions are almost interchangeable.

Against this point of view it could be argued that the mere fact that the jurists went to the trouble of distinguishing the actions shows that they were very different, and the length of the title on the *a.a.p.a.* shows that the difference must have been an important one in practice. We do know of some differences: for example, the servitude action was *in rem*, the *a.a.p.a. in personam*.[2] While the differences may not be of enormous importance, they are

---

[1] The dominant view at present would be that the rigid division of servitudes into rustic and urban is scholastic, dating from about the time of Gaius. See Kaser, 70 (1953) *ZSS* 144 ff. Not all his arguments are acceptable. His account of 50. 16. 198, Ulpian 2 *de omnibus tribunalibus* is vitiated by a failure to note its palingenesia. Lenel, *Pal.* 2, 994. Schulz had spotted this: *Classical Roman Law*, 396. The same error still plagues Grosso, *Servitù*, 137 and 168 n. 2.

[2] 39. 3. 6. 5, Ulpian 53 *ad edictum*. See Lenel, *E.P.* 377 n. 3.

differences and the actions were not one and the same. As long as the two actions existed, it would be necessary to define their areas of application, however little the results may have varied in practice. The *a.a.p.a.* may have continued to thrive because it was an old and well-established action the effects of which were generally understood by lawyers. Nor should the force of legal conservatism be underestimated especially when the new action would not appear to offer any conspicuous advantages. Except perhaps in the opinion of Cassius in 39. 3. 1. 19, there are no signs of any attempt in the classical period to restrict the scope of the *a.a.p.a.* in favour of the *actio negatoria*.

The Requirement of an Opus

One difference between the actions which might be suggested would be the requirement of an *opus* in one and not in the other. It could be argued that for the *a.a.p.a.* the defendant had to have made an *opus*, while he could be liable under the *actio negatoria* even without an *opus*. We saw[1] how Bonfante in disputing with Beseler on 39. 3. 1. 17 put the opposite opinion and said that there had to be an *opus* before the defendant was liable in the *actio negatoria*. Beseler was protesting—and in this he was right—against any idea that an owner could ward off all rain water as *stillicidium* or *flumen*. This is the danger into which a theory of liability without an *opus* could lead, and it is certain that the Romans took the view that a natural flow of water could not be checked—a lower *praedium* had to suffer the water which nature herself sent its way.[2]

---

[1] Above, 151.

[2] The matter is touched on in 39. 3. 1. 22 and 23 which have both been variously challenged but which are hardly to be rejected on this point. If the later parts of 1. 23 are reliable at all, they suggest that although an owner, on to whose land large volumes of water flowed naturally, might not be able to stop this, in certain situations he could have the right to make dams and ditches on his neighbour's land. The authenticity of the account is not beyond doubt. See recently L. Capogrossi Colognesi, *Ricerche sulla struttura delle servitù d'acqua in diritto romano* (Milan, 1966), 175 n. 286 and Nörr, *Die Entstehung*, 49 ff.; Grosso, *Servitù*, 235 ff. See also *Ind. Itp.* and Biondi, *Cat* .143; Sargenti, *L'actio aquae pluviae arcendae* (Milan 1940) 93 n. 3. Attention may be drawn to some remarks on the subject by Daube, 91 (1943) *Law Journal* 180, esp. at 189. He rightly sees the problem as analogous to that of a natural object cutting off a supply of light. The allusion to Swift is pleasing.

The commentaries on the *a.a.p.a.* contain discussion of the requirement of an *opus manu factum*, and despite Sargenti's arguments to the contrary this was always a prerequisite.[1] On the other hand, we hear nothing of any *opus* in the servitude texts. Does this not show that there was the suggested difference? What can be conceded is that there was no requirement of an *opus* as such. That is to say the word *opus* was not a term of art in the servitude action as it was in the *a.a.p.a.*, but this follows purely and simply from the different wordings of the two actions. What cannot be validly deduced is that there was no need of something substantially similar in fact though not in name. The wording of the servitude action itself tells us as much: the defendant does not just 'have' a *flumen* or *stillicidium* on his neighbour's land; he is much more active than that and 'sends in' or 'discharges' (*immittere*) or 'diverts' (*avertere*) the water on to the land. Unfortunately not enough of the commentary has been preserved for us to gauge the exact scope of these words, but they envisage the defendant doing something to alter the offending flow. They are words which are found in passages on the *a.a.p.a.*[2]

One can go further. The commentary on the word *opus* in the *a.a.p.a.* is preserved, especially in 39. 3. 1. 1–1. 15, and we are told distinctly in 1. 14 and 1. 15 that an *opus* is a prerequisite of liability under the *a.a.p.a.* If it were the case that there was no substantially similar requirement for the *actio negatoria* to lie, we should expect to find some mention of its availability in these cases. There is none.

These considerations indicate that there was no significant difference between the *a.a.p.a.* and the *actio negatoria* in this respect. The *actio negatoria* lay only where there was a relevant act of the defendant and this act would often come to much the same as an *opus* in terms of the *a.a.p.a.* Thus despite the lack of direct evidence for the town, we should expect that, just as in the country, an owner would have to tolerate a natural flow of water. Indeed, if he blocked it and as a result the water flowed back on

---

[1] M. Sargenti, *Actio*, 40 ff. Watson, *Property*, 160–9—not all his interpretations are acceptable.
[2] See for *avertere* 39. 3. 1. 18; for *immittere* 39. 3. 1. 1, 3 pr., 11. 5.

to his neighbour's land and did damage there, he would be liable to an action of *stillicidia* and *flumina* himself. At the same time, harm due to a natural flow of water would probably be a less common occurrence in the town, because the conglomeration of buildings would mean that water would seldom run in the courses which nature had laid down for it. Hence an owner would usually have an action.

At the end of the day it seems that in the matters which affect us there were no important differences between the *a.a.p.a.* and the *actio negatoria* of *stillicidia* and *flumina*. They differed chiefly in the locality of their application. In both country and town a man had to suffer a certain amount of water from his neighbour's land and it was only if the water caused him loss that he could bring the appropriate action. The vast gulf which yawns between the country and town systems in Burckhard's account did not exist in classical Roman law.

In 39. 3. 2. 10[1] Paul provides evidence of how the servitude of sending down water was used in practice in the country and this can be used for the town also if the actions are similar. The part of the text in brackets is almost certainly interpolated,[2] but only Solazzi has challenged the rest.[3] His arguments were that no such servitude existed and that the second part of the text should be different from the first but apparently is not. A possible reply to the first point has been outlined already.[4] The second is not an original observation by Solazzi and it has force. The form of the text does make us expect that what Labeo says should be a consequence of what Ofilius says; and yet it is not. Solazzi was inclined to think that Labeo was referring to some real right established by *in iure cessio*, but not a servitude. He does not explain this further and his suggestion is not a happy one. It certainly does not furnish a safe ground for excising the end of the text. Perhaps *cui consequens est* is an ill-chosen piece of abbrevia-

[1] Set out above, 158.
[2] Cf. *Ind. Itp.* and Watson, *Property*, 173 ff. with refs.
[3] *Specie*, 117 ff. His arguments impressed Sargenti, *Studi de Francisci* 3, 352 n. 3.
[4] Above, 156 ff.

tion by the compilers, but that is not a particularly satisfactory solution either.

We have already suggested that the first part may mark the initial stages of accepting that a servitude which had originally applied in the town could be used in the country and would cut off the *a.a.p.a.* If, as was also suggested, the original wording of *stillicidia et flumina* was not well suited to the country and modifications suggested themselves, then Labeo's opinion in the present text may perhaps be explained as a decision on wording. It had been agreed that a servitude could be used in the country and Labeo was saying that it could be set up by the wording *ius ei esse aquam immittere*. Paul approved of this wording.

Whatever the precise meaning of the second sentence, Paul agrees with Ofilius that if a piece of land was burdened with a servitude to receive water, the *a.a.p.a.* was not available. Labeo says something similar. The servitude here must be to enable him to send more than the normal amount. The same must apply to stillicide. There is then room for a servitude *stillicidii non recipiendi*.

The text is not explicit as to precisely why the action is excluded. The previous passage 2. 9 is about *arcere* in the formula and so 2. 10 must be on that word or on *oportere*.[1] I suspect it is on *oportere*, the servitude as a right *in rem* perhaps even affecting the basic situation sufficiently to exclude the *oportere* directly rather than merely to give rise to an *exceptio*. It might even be that the enigmatic doubts of Paul were related to problems of this kind.

Next we come to a text which has been the subject of a vast literature[2] and which raises many problems.

8. 5. 8. 5 Ulpian (17 ad edictum) Aristo Cerellio Vitali respondit non putare se ex taberna casiaria fumum in superiora aedificia iure immitti posse, nisi ei rei servitutem talem admittit. idemque ait: et ex superiore in inferiora non aquam non quid aliud immitti licet: in suo enim alii hactenus facere licet, quatenus nihil in alienum immittat, fumi autem sicut aquae esse immissionem: posse igitur superiorem cum

---

[1] Cf. Lenel, *E.P.* 377.
[2] For refs. *Ind. Itp.* and *Suppl.* along with Kaser, *R.P.R.* 1, 441 n. 8. Watson, *Property*, 177 ff.

inferiore agere ius illi non esse id ita facere. Alfenum denique scribere ait posse ita agi ius illi non esse in suo lapidem caedere ut in meum fundum fragmenta cadant. dicit igitur Aristo eum, qui tabernam casiariam a Minturnensibus conduxit, a superiore prohiberi posse fumum immittere, sed Minturnenses ei ex conducto teneri: agique sic posse dicit cum eo, qui eum fumum immittat, ius ei non esse fumum immittere. ergo per contrarium agi poterit ius esse fumum immittere: quod et ipsum videtur Aristo probare. sed et interdictum uti possidetis poterit locum habere, si quis prohibeatur, qualiter velit, suo uti.

For us only the parts on water are important and these occur in the second sentence. The text will cease to be of direct relevance for classical law if we follow Lenel[1] and Beseler[2] in holding the second sentence to be interpolated—Lenel exempted *idemque ait*. There are many indications that it is at the very least generalized, for example the *quid aliud, et non* instead of *neque*, and the vague *facere licet*. Watson[3] does not assume interpolation. Perhaps Lenel goes too far. We should regard *et ex superiore–immittat* as an addition, but leave the part from *fumi autem* as essentially genuine. Lenel objects to *id ita facere* and would prefer *aedificio suo uti*. Normally such a vague formulation would be suspicious, but not so much here. Aristo is saying that sending smoke above and sending water below are similar and the form of action is the same; he therefore uses these vague colourless words which cover both cases. Lenel also takes the indirect speech here following the direct speech of the rest of the sentence as one of the signs of interpolation; but this may be the wrong way round. After *idemque ait* we expect indirect speech, and it is the surprising fact that what follows is in direct speech which suggests strongly that it is a later addition. When the text reverts to indirect speech this marks a return to the genuine portion. The interpolated part may be no more than an expansion of what Ulpian is telling us and may indeed be in place of some further remarks of his. Yet the interpolation is not quite in harmony with the rest of the text, for it intrudes an over-simplified notion that one should so act *in suo* as

---

[1] 39 (1918) *ZSS* 169. [2] 45 (1938) *BIDR* 173.
[3] *Property*, 177 ff. His exposition does not convince me. I find it hard to believe in any special view of Alfenus on the scope of the *actio negatoria*. Above all, 8. 5. 17. 1, Alfenus 2 *digestorum* has nothing to do with an *actio negatoria*.

to send nothing into one's neighbour's sphere. This crude formulation clashes with the very next text, 8. 5. 8. 6 which says one can make some *non gravem* smoke on one's land and no neighbour may object. Hence no action to assert this right will be given.

If the text is taken in this way,[1] it merely tells us that sending in smoke is similar to sending in water and that an action can be brought denying the right to do it. The smoke involved in the text is not normal smoke but smoke from a cheese factory, smoke which would be particularly obnoxious. We are told that this smoke could be prevented, while 8. 5. 8. 6 and 7 also suggest that the aim was to deal with excesses. Taken within this framework the remark on water would indicate that the classical *actio negatoria* was available to prevent an excessive flow of water. It was only some later, possibly Justinianic, jurist who wrote the rather less subtle remarks which make up the interpolated section.

Finally, 39. 3. 3 pr. is frequently cited in connection with the *actio negatoria*,[2] but it is a discussion of the term *aqua pluvia* in the formula of the *a.a.p.a.* and is not relevant to the present discussion.[3]

The aim of this chapter has been to show that the situation was that a man had to tolerate a certain amount of water from his neighbour's land. This was the case with the *a.a.p.a.* and we have no reason for thinking it was different where the *actio negatoria* applied. If that was so, then the two servitudes mentioned in the texts could have existed: *stillicidii recipiendi* to receive more than

---

[1] As it is apparently by the standard books, Kaser, *R.P.R.* 1, 441 n. 8. Jörs-Kunkel, *Römisches Privatrecht*, 125 n.7.

[2] For instance Jörs-Kunkel, *Römisches Privatrecht*, 125 n. 7; E. Rabel, *Grundzüge des römischen Privatrechts* (2nd edition, Basel, 1955), 55.

[3] See Rodger, 38 (1970) *Tijd.* 417. In addition to the discussion there, it may be noted that 39. 3. 3 pr. and 1, Ulpian 53 *ad edictum* are strangely situated in the Digest. They are comments on the term *aqua pluvia* and yet form part of a paragraph 39. 3. 3 which ends up in 3. 3 and 3. 4 with remarks relating to the parties to an action—3. 4 is at best some sort of an abbreviation (perhaps of a text which originally stood between 3 and 4, since the consecutive fragments from the same book of Ulpian indicate an omission.) The simplest way to take 3. 2 is as something to do with the class of exempted agricultural *opera*. We must then sever 3 pr.—3. 2 from 3. 3 and 3. 4. This is, of course, what Lenel does (*Pal.* 2, 755), but we are then left with 3 pr.—3. 2 as comments which have gone astray. 3 pr.—3. 1 should be replaced between 1. 15 and 1. 16 as part of the commentary which the compilers cut out. See above, 155. 3. 2 should be put somewhere in 1. 3—1. 9.

the usual amount, and *stillicidii non recipiendi* to free an owner from the necessity of receiving any at all. This solution is similar to that proposed for the analogous problem of lights.

It is not proposed to elaborate on matters of formulae or procedure. For one thing the material is lacking; for another, if the scheme for light was acceptable, a similar one could doubtless be worked out to cover stillicide. Without texts to back it up it would be hypothetical and could claim plausibility only to the extent that it reflected what was plausible for lights. Such an unrewarding task is best left unperformed.

INDEX OF TEXTS